Listen Up! MATH

Activities to Improve Math and Listening Skills

Can you find 16 ladybugs in this book, including me?

by Ann Richmond Fisher

illustrated by Bron Smith

Teaching & Learning Company

1204 Buchanan St., P.O. Box 10
Carthage, IL 62321

Cover by Bron Smith

Copyright © 1994, Teaching & Learning Company

ISBN No. 1-57310-005-6

Printing No. 9876

Teaching & Learning Company
1204 Buchanan St., P.O. Box 10
Carthage, IL 62321

This book belongs to

_____

Dedication

This book is lovingly dedicated
to my twenty-one nieces and nephews
and to those who are yet to be added
to this delightful group.

Table of Contents

Dear Teacher,

How many times have your students had to redo assignments because they didn't *listen* to the directions? How many times have you had to repeat yourself unnecessarily? How often have you wished you could take time out from your regular lessons to work just on listening? This book was written to help you solve these problems. *Listening and following directions* are the focus of this book. The mastery of these two key skills is crucial to the success of every student *and* every adult. An important bonus of this book is that you don't have to take time away from other meaningful work while building listening skills. While your students are becoming better listeners, they are also practicing valuable math skills.

This book is a complete resource for the busy teacher. It contains everything from pretests to a chart for recording student progress to student award certificates. The lessons were also designed with the busy teacher in mind. For many of the lessons, your students will need only a piece of paper and pencil. For others you will need to photocopy a reproducible page and supply crayons or rulers. Materials needed are always listed in the top corner of the lesson. An answer key is provided in the back of the book which will often help you check students' work with a glance. (It should be noted that in some cases students' answers can vary slightly from the answer key and still be acceptable.)

The math lessons are arranged by topic as listed in the table of contents. In general, easier lessons are placed first in each section. The skills covered are also listed in the top corner of each lesson for your quick reference. It is suggested that you begin with easier lessons that contain math skills with which your students are already very familiar, so that the focus will be on *listening*. You may also want to repeat directions two or three times in the beginning and then gradually move towards both harder skills and less teacher help.

The section that follows, "How to Use This Book," contains more specific instructions on using special features of the book such as the Pre/Posttests and Warm-Ups. It is our goal to help you, the classroom teacher, improve the listening skills of your students in an easy, enjoyable manner!

Sincerely,

Ann

Ann Richmond Fisher

How to Use This Book

To get maximum benefit from the various features of this book, use the suggestions that follow.

Warm-Ups: These are fun activities at the beginning of each section that will introduce students to the upcoming content area. The purpose of the warm-ups is not only to give students a sample of the work ahead, but also to get students excited about it.

Pre/Posttests: These have been written to help the teacher evaluate student progress. The teacher should carefully preview the upcoming unit before administering the pretest. If some lessons are inappropriate for your class (i.e. too difficult or too easy), then there may also be inappropriate items on the pre/posttest. Feel free to use only the questions on the tests that correspond to lessons in the unit you will actually be using. Come up with your own number for the highest possible test score. Use the **Teacher Record Page** to record the date of each pretest, the number of items on the test and each student's score. After the class completes all appropriate lessons in the unit, administer the same test again, and record student scores for the posttest on the record page. At a glance you can see which students are making significant progress in their listening and math skills. If some students are not improving, try to work with them individually or in small groups to diagnose any problems they may be having.

Lessons: Most lessons are written so that you can read them to an entire class while each student completes one page of work. You can then collect the work and evaluate it using the **Answer Key** in the back of the book. Or students can check their own work as the entire class works through the correct solution together. IMPORTANT: In each lesson students are instructed where to write their names on the paper. Make sure they wait and listen to these instructions. Also note that for some lessons such as "Fraction Draw" (page 71) and "Home Improvements" (page 73), students' answers can vary slightly and still be correct. Shapes can be divided differently, features can be combined differently, and so on.

Although the lessons can be administered in a traditional manner described above, some can also be adapted to other formats. A few ideas are listed below. Feel free to use your imagination and try other ideas of your own.

Chalkboard Lessons: "One to Ten" (page 3), "What's Missing?" (page 31), "Score More" (page 35), "Time to Draw" (page 56) and many others written on plain paper can be done at the chalkboard. You may wish to have three or four students at the chalkboard while the rest work at their seats. This allows you to spot problems immediately. The chalkboard workers may be distracting to the others; students will need to listen and concentrate even harder. They may need to be reminded that other answers may be possible, or that other answers may be incorrect. Emphasize the need for each child to do his own best work.

Teamwork: Some of the story problems such as "Baseball" (page 30), "Adam's Apples" (page 34), "Scoreboard" (page 40) and "Betsy's Birthday" (page 63) can be done in small groups. This requires students to agree on what they've heard and to work cooperatively on a solution.

Team Relays: Combining both ideas above, some activities could be done at the board by teams working in a relay fashion. "Numbered Boxes" (page 11) and "Line Up" (page 50) could be done in this manner. Divide the class into teams of four to six students each. One member from each team would go to the chalkboard and follow one portion of instructions, the next member would do the next portion, etc. All along the way, the team would need to listen carefully to be sure instructions were being followed. Someone from each team could be given the opportunity to correct mistakes made earlier.

Teacher Record Page

Student Name	# possible	Pretest 1	Posttest 1	Pretest 2	Posttest 2	Pretest 3	Posttest 3	Pretest 4	Posttest 4	Pretest 5	Posttest 5	Pretest 6	Posttest 6
Date													

Materials:
Reproducible on page 2
Pencil

Numbers, Counting and Place Value

1. Write your name on the top right corner of your page.

2. Count the apples in row A. Write the number that tells how many apples there are in the blank.

3. In row A, circle the third apple.

4. Put an *X* on the second apple in row A.

5. In row B, underline the number 8.

6. In row B, put an *X* on the number 4.

7. In row C, find the jar with the most jelly beans. Circle it.

8. In row C, find the 2 jars with the same number of jelly beans. Underline them.

9. In row D, write these numbers as I read them to you:
   9, 12, 3, 25, 36, 17, 48.

10. In row E, write the numbers I leave out while counting from 1 to 20.
    1, 3, 4, 5, 7, 8, 10, 11, 13, 14, 16, 17, 19, 20.

11. In row F, circle the number with 2 tens.
    Underline the number with 6 ones.
    Put an *X* on the number with a 1 in the hundreds place.

12. In row G, write the largest even number from this list:
    64, 71, 67, 66, 63.

Numbers, Counting and Place Value

A.  _____

B. 7   4   8   2   3   6

C.

D.

E.

F. 36   129   71   4   265

G.

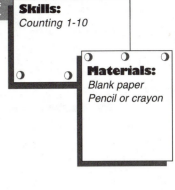

Skills:
Counting 1–10

Materials:
Blank paper
Pencil or crayon

One to Ten

Use as a Warm-Up for Part 1.

1. Write your name one time at the top of your paper.

2. Draw 2 lines under your name.

3. Draw 3 apples with stems.

4. Add 2 leaves to each stem so that you have 6 leaves altogether.

5. Write 5 As under your apples.

6. Circle 4 of the As.

7. On the back of your paper draw 8 pies.

8. Draw a line under 7 of the pies.

9. Draw 10 happy faces under the pies.

10. Draw hats on 9 of the heads.

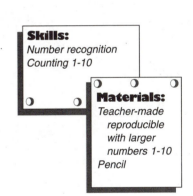

Skills:
Number recognition
Counting 1–10

Materials:
Teacher-made
reproducible
with larger
numbers 1–10
Pencil

Find the Number

1. Find the number 4 and draw a ring around it.

2. Draw 6 dots under the number 6.

3. Draw a line to connect the numbers 1 and 5.

4. Draw 2 lines under the number 2.

5. Put an X on the number 10.

6. Draw a box around the number 8.

7. Draw 1 line on top of the number 9.

8. Draw 3 balls under the number 3.

9. Draw 1 wiggly line under the number 7.

10. Write your name above the number 1.

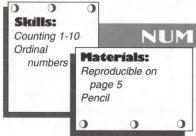

Skills:
Counting 1-10
Ordinal numbers

Materials:
Reproducible on page 5
Pencil

Window Shopping

1. Find the store with 9 windows. Write your name on the roof. You will start your shopping trip here.

2. Secondly, go to the store with 5 windows. Draw a line from the first store to the second store.

3. Next, visit the store with 10 windows. Draw a line from the second store to the third store.

4. Fourthly, go to the store with 4 windows. Draw a line from the third store to the fourth store.

5. Next, visit the store with 7 windows. Draw a line from the fourth store to the fifth store.

6. Lastly, go to the store with 8 windows. Draw a line from the fifth store to the sixth store.

7. Do not go to the store with 6 windows. Draw an *X* on the roof of the store with 6 windows.

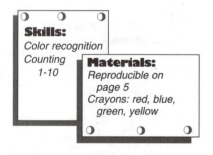

Skills:
Color recognition
Counting 1-10

Materials:
Reproducible on page 5
Crayons: red, blue, green, yellow

Colored Windows

1. Find the store with 8 windows. Color all the windows in this store red.

2. Find the store with 10 windows. Color 5 of these windows blue. Color the other 5 yellow.

3. Find the store with 7 windows. Color the roof of this store green.

4. Find the store with 6 windows. Color the door on this store red.

5. Find the store with 9 windows. Write your name on the roof of this store.

6. Find the store with 4 windows. Color the roof of this store blue.

7. Find the store with 5 windows. Color the roof of this store yellow.

Windows

Reproducible for use with listening lessons on page 4.

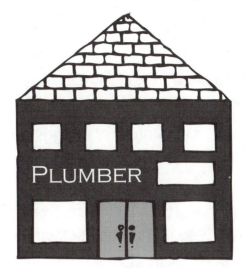

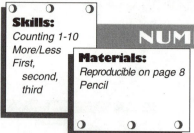

Skills:
Counting 1-10
More/Less
First,
    second,
    third

Materials:
Reproducible on page 8
Pencil

Egg Count 1

1. Count the eggs in the first nest. Circle the number under the nest that tells how many are in the nest.

2. Now count the eggs in each basket. Circle the numbers under the baskets that tell how many eggs are in each basket.

3. Find the basket with the same number of eggs as the first nest. Draw a line to connect them.

4. Count the eggs in the second nest.
   If there are *less* eggs than in the first nest, cross out the nest.
   If there are *more* eggs than in the first nest, circle the nest.

5. Now count the eggs in the third nest.
   Again, if there are *less* eggs than in the first nest, cross out the nest.
   If there are *more* eggs than in the first nest, circle the nest.

6. Write your name above the nests.

Skills:
*Adding to make 10
Most/Fewest*

Materials:
*Reproducible on
page 8
Pencil or crayon*

Egg Count 2

1. Count the number of eggs in the first nest.
   Circle the number underneath that tells how many eggs
   are in the nest.

2. For the second and third nests, count the eggs.
   In the bottom part of each nest, write the number that tells how many eggs
   are in that nest.

3. Draw a line under the nest with the fewest eggs.

4. Circle the nest with the most eggs. Now add more eggs
   to this nest so that there are 10 eggs altogether.
   Write the number of eggs you added *above* that nest.

5. Now count the number of eggs in each basket.
   Circle the number under each one that
   tells how many eggs are in the baskets.

6. Write your name on the basket with the fewest number of eggs.

7. Circle the basket with the most eggs.
   Add more eggs to this basket so that there are 10 eggs altogether.
   Write the number of eggs you added on the front of the basket.

...three...

Z
Z
Z
Z
z

Eggs

Reproducible for use with listening lessons on pages 6 and 7.

4 5 6 7

4 5 6 7

4 5 6 7

4 5 6 7

4 5 6 7

Colored Clues

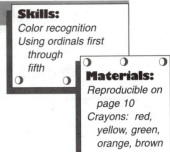

Skills:
Color recognition
Using ordinals first through fifth

Materials:
Reproducible on page 10
Crayons: red, yellow, green, orange, brown

1. In the second row, color the third arrow orange.

2. In the fourth row, color the first dog brown.

3. In the fifth row, color the second moon green.

4. In the first row, color the third ball red.

5. In the third row, color the first bat brown.

6. In the fourth row, color the fifth picture yellow.

7. In the fifth row, color the second picture orange.

8. In the second row, color the fourth arrow red.

9. In the first row, color the second apple green.

10. In the third row, color the fifth picture orange.

11. In the fifth row, color the third star yellow.

12. In the fourth row, color the first cat brown.

13. In the third row, color the third bat yellow.

14. In the second row, color the fifth arrow orange.

15. Write your name under the box of pictures. Circle the first letter of your name.

Rows of Pictures

Reproducible for use with listening lessons on pages 9 and 27.

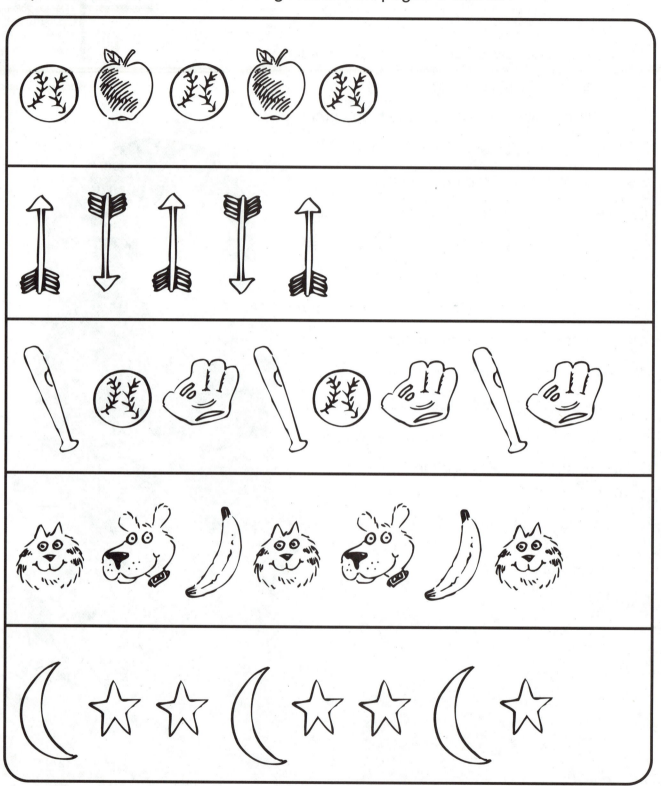

umbered oxes

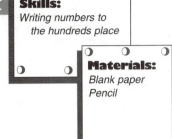

Skills:
*Writing numbers to
the hundreds place*

Materials:
*Blank paper
Pencil*

1. Write your name in the upper right-hand corner of your paper.

2. Now draw 6 boxes on your paper.
   They need to be large enough so that several numbers
   can be written inside.
   First make one row of 3 boxes going across your paper.
   Under that row make a second row with 3 more boxes.

3. Next you will label the boxes.
   Write a number in the upper left-hand corner of each box.
   Start with the top left box and label it with the number 1.
   Move one box to the right and label it 2.
   The last box in the top row will be labelled with a 3.
   Go to the second row, start at the left and label those boxes 4, 5 and 6.

4. Next I will read some numbers. Write each number inside
   the box or boxes that have the same digits as the number I read.
   For example, if I read the number 19, you would write it
   in the 1 box because it has a 1. If I read the number 24,
   you would write it in the 2 box and the 4 box. If I read the number 97,
   you would not write it anywhere. (Repeat these directions.)

5. Here are the numbers:
   27, 18, 36, 94, 88, 65, 47, 28, 51, 32, 79, 146, 329, 542.

6. Now circle the box with the most numbers.

(Teacher: This can be easily adapted with larger or smaller numbers. Also, boxes
can be labelled with different numbers.)

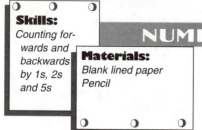

Skills:
Counting forwards and backwards by 1s, 2s and 5s

Materials:
Blank lined paper
Pencil

NUMBERS, COUNTING AND PLACE VALUE

Count Up, Count Down

(Teacher: You may wish to select only the items from this page that are most appropriate to ability level of your students. These items can also be adapted.)

1. Write your name in the top left corner of your paper.

2. I'm going to count from 1 to 20 and leave out some numbers.
   On the first line of your paper, write down all the numbers I leave out.
   1, 2, 3, 4, 5, 7, 8, 9, 10, 11, 12, 14, 16, 17, 19, 20.

3. Now I will count from 1 to 50. On the next line of your paper, write down all the numbers that I miss. Use an extra line if you need it.
   1, 2, 3, 5, 6, 7, 9, 10, 11, 12, 14, 15, 16, 18, 19, 20, 22, 23, 24, 26, 27, 28, 29, 30
   31, 33, 34, 35, 37, 38, 39, 41, 42, 43, 45, 46, 48, 49, 50.

4. Next I will start at 50 and count by 2s to 100.
   List the numbers that I leave out.
   50, 52, 54, 58, 60, 64, 66, 68, 72, 74, 76, 80, 82, 86, 88, 92, 94, 98, 100.

5. I will count to 100 by 5s and leave out some numbers.
   Please write down the numbers I miss.
   5, 10, 15, 20, 30, 35, 40, 45, 55, 60, 70, 75, 80, 85, 95, 100.

6. I will count down from 20 to 1. Write down the numbers I leave out.
   20, 19, 17, 16, 14, 13, 12, 10, 9, 7, 6, 5, 3, 2, 1.

7. Now I will count down from 100 to 1 by 5s.
   List the numbers that I leave out.
   100, 90, 85, 80, 70, 65, 60, 55, 45, 40, 35, 30, 25, 15, 10, 5.

8. Finally, I will count down from 50 to 0 by 2s.
   Write down the numbers that I skip.
   50, 48, 44, 42, 38, 36, 34, 30, 28, 24, 22, 20, 16, 14, 10, 8, 4, 2, 0.

Number Hunt 1

Skills:
Number recognition
1-50

Materials:
Reproducible on
page 15 (Cover
or remove bot-
tom half of chart)
Pencil or crayon

1. Put an *X* on these numbers: 4, 12, 25, 38, 47.

2. Circle these numbers: 19, 37, 6, 45, 23.

3. Draw lines under these numbers: 39, 24, 8, 31, 48, 14.

4. Shade in the boxes that contain these numbers: 7, 41, 16, 26.

5. Draw lines to connect these number pairs: 3 and 13, 32 and 41, 39 and 50, 18 and 29.

6. Write your name in the upper right corner of your page.

Number Hunt 2

1. Put an *X* on every number with 6 ones.

2. Circle every number with 4 tens.

3. Shade in the boxes that contain these numbers: 78, 35, 91, 52, 17, 20, 28.

4. Underline the number that is more than 82 and less than 84.

5. Underline the number that is less than 76 and more than 74.

6. Draw a line above the number that is more than 11 and less than 13.

7. Draw a line above the number that is less than 98 and more than 96.

8. Write your name below the chart.

NUMBER HUNT

Number Chart

Reproducible for use with pages 13, 14 and 52.

1	2	3	4	5	6	7	8	9	10
11	12	13	14	15	16	17	18	19	20
21	22	23	24	25	26	27	28	29	30
31	32	33	34	35	36	37	38	39	40
41	42	43	44	45	46	47	48	49	50
51	52	53	54	55	56	57	58	59	60
61	62	63	64	65	66	67	68	69	70
71	72	73	74	75	76	77	78	79	80
81	82	83	84	85	86	87	88	89	90
91	92	93	94	95	96	97	98	99	100

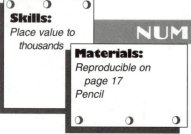

Columns

1. In column A, circle the lowest number.

2. In column D, circle the highest number.

3. Circle the letter of the column where the numbers are in order from smallest to largest.

4. In column D, draw a line under the lowest number.

5. In column B, circle the 2 numbers that have the same value in the ones place.

6. In column A, draw an *X* on the number with the most tens.

7. In column C, draw an *X* on the number with the lowest value in the tens place.

8. In column B, draw 2 dots under the number with the lowest value.

9. Put a line above all numbers on this page that have 6 hundreds.

10. Find the only number that has a 1 in the thousands place and draw a wiggly line under it.

11. Find the largest number on the entire page and draw a dark box around it.

12. Write your name at the top of the page.

Columns

Reproducible for use with page 16.

A	B	C	D
346	43	54	604
68	5128	72	2137
97	963	530	695
1401	6	2695	628

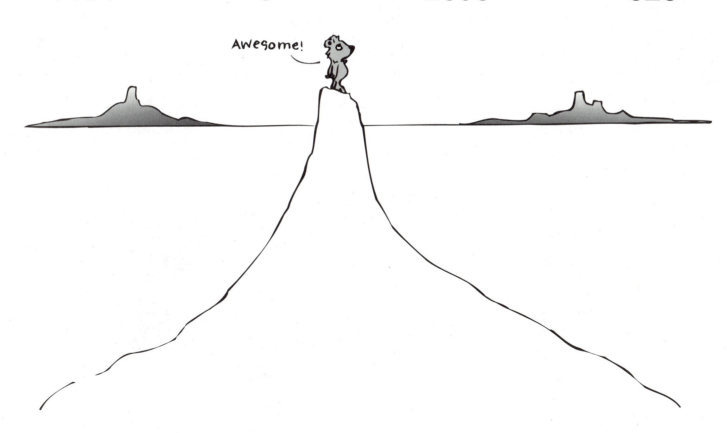

Awesome!

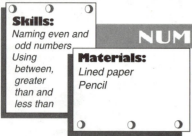

Skills:
Naming even and odd numbers Using between, greater than and less than

Materials:
Lined paper
Pencil

NUMBERS, COUNTING AND PLACE VALUE

Even—Odd

Number the lines on your paper from 1 to 12. Write the answers to each set of directions on the correct line.

1. Write all the odd numbers that are less than 6.

2. Write all the even numbers between 11 and 19.

3. Write 3 even numbers that are greater than 20 but less than 28.

4. Write 5 odd numbers that are less than 50 but greater than 40.

5. Write 2 odd numbers between 95 and 100.

6. Write 4 even numbers less than 20.

7. Write 3 odd numbers between 80 and 90.

8. Write the largest even number from this list: 16, 27, 35, 8, 26, 31.

9. Write the smallest even number from this list: 72, 75, 87, 82, 86.

10. Write the smallest odd number from this list: 21, 13, 4, 7, 15, 20.

11. Write the largest odd number from this list: 94, 91, 92, 88, 89, 90.

12. Write your first name and your last name in this space. If both names together have an odd number of letters, underline your name. If both names together have an even number of letters, circle your name.

Shapes and Patterns

Materials:
*Reproducible on
page 20
Pencil*

1. In line A, shade the small circle with your pencil.

2. In line A, underline the triangle.

3. In line A, write your name in the rectangle.

4. Look at the animal in line B. Count the number of squares used to make the animal. Write the number that tells how many inside the square next to the animal.

5. Count how many rectangles are in the animal. Write the number of rectangles you see inside the rectangle on the side.

6. Listen to this pattern. Draw the shape that comes next on line C.
   circle, square, circle, square, _____

7. Next to that shape, draw the number that comes next in this pattern.
   7, 1, 9, 7, 1, 9, 7, _____

8. On line D, write the numbers that are missing from this pattern.
   2, 4, 6, 8, 12, 14, 16, 20.

9. In the space labelled E, follow these instructions: Draw a triangle in the bottom right corner of your space. Draw a square in the top left corner. Draw a circle in the bottom left corner. Draw a dotted line to connect the triangle and the square.

Shapes and Patterns

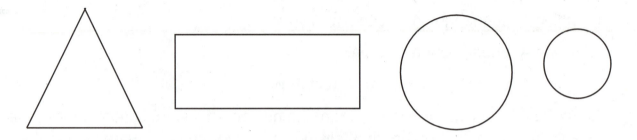

A.

B.

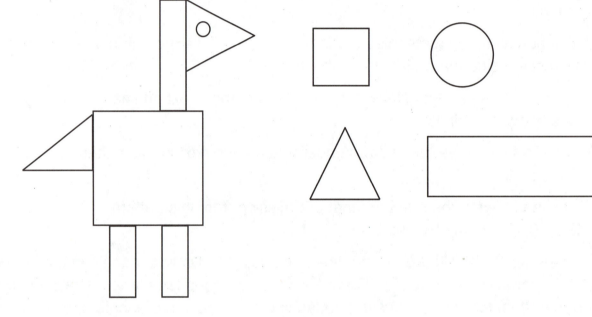

C. _____   D. _____

E.

Clown Face

Skills:
Drawing shapes
Counting 1-5

Materials:
Blank paper
Pencil

Use as a Warm-Up for Part 2.

Let's draw a clown face. Please follow these directions.

1. Make a large circle for the clown's head.

2. Now make a smaller circle inside the large one for the clown's nose.

3. Draw 2 small triangles for the clown's eyes. Then draw a larger triangle around each small one to make the eyes bigger.

4. Add a great big smile and 2 large ears.

5. Add a triangle-shaped hat. Decorate it by drawing 5 small squares inside.

6. Add some curly hair around the clown's hat. Write your name under the clown.

Act It Out!

Skills:
Imitating patterns
Left/Right

Materials:
Just students

Use as Warm-Up for Part 2.

Here are a few ideas to fill in spare moments at the end of the day, while waiting in line, etc. Use one or more at a time; vary according to the ability of your group. Demonstrate each pattern once or twice, then have students join in. Number in ( ) indicates how many elements are in each pattern. "Snap" = Snap your fingers; "Head," "Shoulder," etc. = Touch that body part.

(2) 1. clap, clap, snap, clap, clap, snap, . . .

(3) 2. raise your right arm, raise your left arm, clap behind your back, . . .

(3) 3. clap, snap, elbows, clap, snap, elbows, . . .

(3) 4. hop on right foot, hop on left foot, take a big step, . . .

(4) 5. turn to the left, pat your head, turn to the right, rub your tummy, . . .

(4) 6. head, knees, elbows, shoulders, . . .

(4) 7. jump, clap, slap your knees, snap, . . .

(4) 8. "cluck" your tongue, pinch your nose, pull your ear, stomp your feet, . . .

(5) 9. stand up, stomp left foot, stomp right foot, sit down, clap, . . .

(5) 10. snap, clap, slap your knees, touch your head, wiggle your nose, . . .

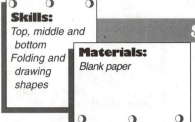

Skills:
Top, middle and bottom
Folding and drawing shapes

Materials:
Blank paper

Folded Shapes

1. Fold your paper in half so you have a rectangle.

2. Turn your paper so that your rectangle is *tall* (so that it goes up and down).

3. At the top of your rectangle, write your name. Under your name draw 4 small circles.

4. In the middle of your paper draw 3 triangles.

5. At the bottom of your paper draw 2 large squares.

6. Now turn your tall rectangle over so you can't see what you wrote. Next, fold the bottom edge of your paper up to the top edge.

7. Finally, turn your paper over again so your name is at the top.

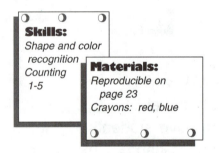

Skills:
Shape and color recognition
Counting 1-5

Materials:
Reproducible on page 23
Crayons: red, blue

Shape Caper

1. Color the small circle red.

2. Color the large triangle blue.

3. Draw 2 blue *X*s in the large square.

4. Put a blue line under the small rectangle.

5. Draw a red ring around the small square.

6. Put 5 dots inside the large rectangle.

7. Put a blue *X* on the small triangle.

8. Write your name inside the large circle.

Shape Caper

Reproducible for use with page 22.

23

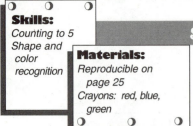
Shape Search

Skills:
Counting to 5
Shape and color recognition

Materials:
Reproducible on page 25
Crayons: red, blue, green

1. Look at the picture of the robot. Count the rectangles.
   Draw a ring around the number that tells how many rectangles you see.

2. In the robot, color all the rectangles red. Color all the triangles blue.

3. Find the square on the robot. Write the letter *S* on this square.

4. Look at the house. Count the circles. Draw a ring around the number that tells how many circles you see.

5. Color the triangle on the house green.

6. Look at the boat. Count the triangles. Draw a ring around the number that tells how many triangles you see.

7. On the boat, color the squares red. Color the circles blue.

8. Look at the tree. Count the circles. Draw a ring around the number that tells how many circles you see.

9. Color the squares on the tree green. Color the rectangle blue.
   Color the circles red.

10. Write your name above the house.

11. Turn your paper over. Draw a circle, a triangle, a square and a rectangle.
    Try to make one or more of your shapes into a picture.

Shape Art

Reproducible for use with pages 23 and 26.

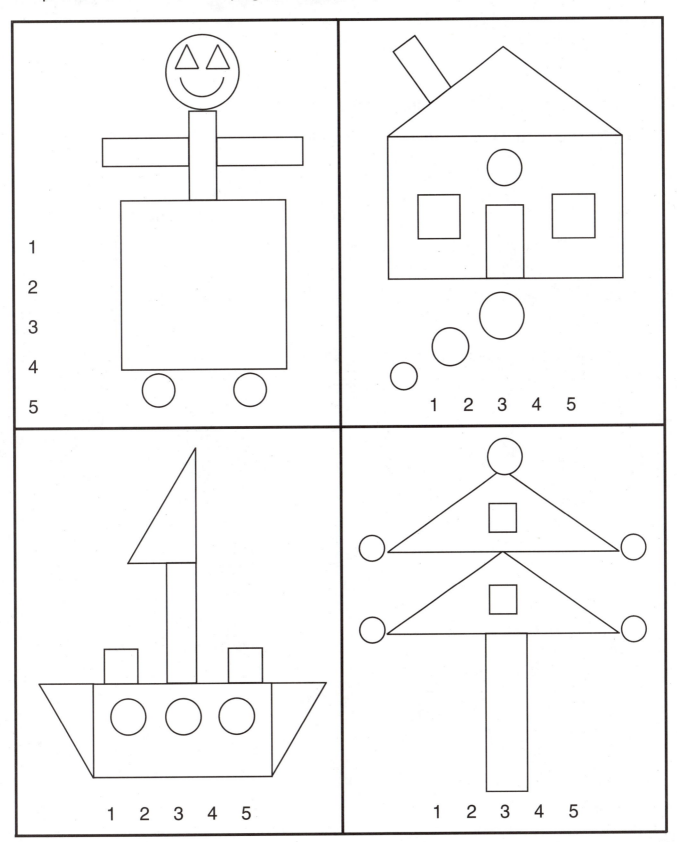

Shapely Details

1. Write your name above the house.

2. Find the picture with 1 triangle. Write the letter *T* on that triangle.

3. Find the 2 pictures on this page that have the same number of circles.
   Draw a line under those 2 pictures.

4. Find the 3 pictures that have the same number of squares.
   For each of these pictures, circle the number that tells how many squares.

5. Find the 2 pictures that have the same number of triangles.
   Put an *X* in the boxes with these pictures.

6. Find the 2 pictures that have the same number of rectangles.
   Put a star in these 2 boxes.

7. Find the picture with the most circles. Shade in these circles with your pencil.

Colored Patterns

Skills:
Identifiying, coloring and extending patterns

Materials:
*Reproducible on page 10
Crayons: red, blue, black, brown, yellow*

1. In the first row, color the balls blue. Color the apples red. Draw what comes next. Color it the right color.

2. In the second row, draw what comes next. Choose 2 of your crayons to color the arrows in a pattern.

3. In the third row, cross out the picture that doesn't fit the pattern.

4. In the fourth row, color the cats brown, the dogs black and the bananas yellow. Draw what comes next. Color it the right color.

5. In the fifth row, color the moons blue and the stars yellow. Draw what comes next. Color it the right color.

6. Put your name on the top of the paper.

Banana Boat

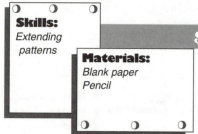

Skills:
Extending patterns

Materials:
Blank paper
Pencil

What's Next?

In this lesson, I want you to listen for patterns. I will read each pattern list two times and ask you to write or draw what comes next.

1. circle, square, circle, square, circle, _____

2. tree, flower, tree, flower, _____

3. star, moon, sun, star, moon, _____

4. 1, 2, 3, 1, 2, 3, 1, _____

5. apple, ball, cow, apple, ball, cow, apple, _____

6. 2, 4, 6, 2, 4, 6, _____

7. cat, dog, bird, cat, dog, bird, _____

8. B, L, F, B, L, F, B, _____

9. shoe, sock, hat, mitten, shoe, sock, hat, mitten, shoe, sock, _____

10. Write a pattern using your first, last and middle names.

Folding Fun

Skills:
Shape recognition
Optional: multiplication,
  addition
Folding
Counting

Materials:
Blank paper
Pencil
Crayons: red,
  orange, yellow,
  green

1. Fold one corner of your paper up and make a crease.

2. Continue folding corners or edges up, making a firm crease each time.
   Fold your paper any way you wish, but try not to fold it in half.
   Put about 7 or 8 folds in your paper altogether.

3. Now spread your paper out flat. You should see several different shapes.

4. Count the number of sides you see in each shape.
   Write that number inside each shape.

5. With your crayons, color the shapes as follows: 3-sided shapes in yellow,
   4-sided shapes in red, 5-sided shapes in green, 6-sided shapes in orange.

6. Count the number of shapes you have of each color. Find which color fills the
   most shapes.

7. With that color, write your name on the back of your paper.

Optional Extra Activity for Older Students:

8. Suppose each shape is worth 1 point per side. For instance, each triangle is
   worth 3 points. Find your total score for this page. First multiply the number of
   triangles you have by 3. Then multiply to find how many points you have in 4-
   sided shapes, 5-sided shapes, etc. Add the totals for each shape together to get
   your final score. Write your score on the back of your paper under your name.
   Compare your score to others in your class.

Skills:
Drawing shapes
Listening
 for details

Materials:
Blank paper
Pencil

S H A P E S   A N D   P A T T E R N S

Baseball

Listen carefully to this story. I will ask you to draw some shapes at different points in the story. Start by drawing a square near the upper left corner of your paper. This represents Bryce's house.

Bryce woke up. It was a beautiful day. "What a great day for baseball!" he thought.

He walked out of his house and remembered he had left his baseball outside the night before. He walked halfway around his house, found the ball, and continued walking around the house just to be sure he hadn't left anything else. Now draw a *dotted path* to show where Bryce walked. Add a *circle* on the path to show where he found the baseball.

Next, Bryce took a diagonal path from his house to the baseball diamond, which is located near the bottom right of your paper. Draw the baseball *diamond*, and draw a *dotted path* to show how Bryce walked there.

Bryce was the first batter. He noticed that home plate was a *pentagon*–a five-sided shape. Draw home plate at the bottom point of your diamond.

Bryce was really fired up. He sent the first pitch out of the field into the bleachers! Draw a *rectangle* above the top point of the diamond to show where the bleachers were. Draw a *circle* in the *rectangle* to show where Bryce's ball landed.

After the game, Bryce headed to the pond. Draw an *oval* to represent the pond near the bottom left corner of your paper. Draw a *dotted path* to show where Bryce walked from the ball diamond to the pond. Bryce met two friends at the pond who were trying out their homemade sailboats. Draw two *triangles* in the pond to represent the sail-boats.

Next, Bryce walked diagonally to the store near the top right corner of your paper. Draw a *rectangle* to show where the store was. Write your name inside the store. Draw a *dotted path* to show where Bryce walked from the pond to the store. Then draw a *dotted path* to show how he walked straight home from the store.

The End

What's Missing?

Skills:
Sequences
Multiples
Calendar

Materials:
Blank paper
Pencil

Number your paper from 1 to 10. Write the numbers in a column down the left side of your paper. On each line, write the word or number missing in each pattern. Sometimes there will be more than one item missing. I will read each pattern twice.

1. 2, 4, 6, 8, 10, 14, 16, 18, 20

2. 5, 10, 15, 20, 30, 35, 45, 50

3. January, February, March, May, June, July, August, September, November, December

4. 1, 3, 5, 7, 9, 13, 15, 19, 21, 23, 25

5. Sunday, Monday, Tuesday, Wednesday, Friday, Saturday

6. ones, tens, thousands, ten thousands

7. first, second, third, fourth, fifth, seventh, eighth, ninth, tenth

8. 20, 19, 18, 16, 15, 14, 12, 11, 10

9. pennies, nickels, quarters, half dollars, dollars

10. 100, 95, 90, 85, 75, 70, 60, 55, 50

11. Write your name in the top right corner.

Materials:
Lined paper
Pencil

Addition and Subtraction

Write your name in the top right corner of the page. Number your paper from 1 to 10. Write the numbers in a column down the left side of your paper. Leave three lines blank for numbers 8, 9 and 10.

1. I will read 3 problems to you. Write just the answers to these problems in order on line 1. 1 + 1, 3 - 2, 2 + 3

2. Listen to this story about Popsicles™. At the end I will ask you to write down how many Popsicles™ Cathy has.
Story: Cathy found 3 Popsicles™ in her freezer. She gave one to her neighbor and ate one herself. Then her mom found 3 more and gave them to Cathy. How many Popsicles™ did Cathy have then? Write your answer on line 2.

3. Write down these number pairs on line 3: 6 and 4, 5 and 4, 3 and 8. Circle the pair that adds up to ten.

4. I will read you 2 math problems. Write down the answer only to the problem with the highest sum. 7 + 6 and 9 + 5 Write your answer on line 4.

5. I will read 3 subtraction problems to you. Write the answers to these in order on line 5. 15 - 7, 16 - 8, 18 - 9

6. Last year there were 19 second grade students. This year there are 15. Did the number of students go up or down? By how much? On line 6, write the word *up* or *down* and the number for your answer.

7. Listen to learn how many goals the Icers scored in a hockey game. Write your answer on line 7. In the first period the Icers score 3 goals. In the second period they score no goals. In the third period they scored 2 goals. In the last period they scored 2 again. How many goals did they score altogether? Write your answer. If their opponents, the Sticks, score 8 goals, which team won the game? Also on line 7, write *I* if the Icers won the game or *S* if the Sticks won the game.

8. Write this subtraction problem in vertical form on line 8 of your paper: 96 - 34 = 52. If the answer is correct, circle it. If the answer is incorrect, put an *X* on it.

9. Copy these 3 numbers on line 9: 529, 241, 706. Write an addition problem. Add the highest number and the lowest number. Write the problem in vertical form and your answer on your paper.

10. Write these 2 problems in vertical form on your paper: 863 - 529 and 617 - 132. Put an *X* next to the problem you think will have the highest answer. Then solve both problems.

Clap It!

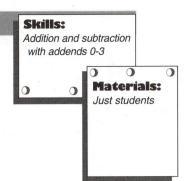

Skills:
Addition and subtraction with addends 0-3

Materials:
Just students

Use as a Warm-Up for Part 3.

I am going to read some addition problems to you.   I want you to clap out the answer. For example, if the answer is two, clap your hands two times. Here we go.

1. 1 + 1	2. 0 + 1	3. 2 + 1
4. 3 + 0	5. 2 + 2	6. 2 + 0
7. 3 + 1	8. 3 + 3	9. 2 + 3

Next I will read some subtraction problems to you. This time, I want you to stomp out the answer with your feet.

10. 2 - 1	11. 1 - 1	12. 3 - 1
13. 3 - 0	14. 2 - 2	15. 3 - 2

Now I will read addition *and* subtraction problems. Listen carefully! If the problem is addition, clap the answer. If the problem is subtraction, stomp the answer.

16. 2 + 1	17. 3 - 2	18. 2 - 1
19. 1 + 3	20. 1 + 1	21. 3 - 0
22. 2 + 2	23. 3 - 1	24. 2 + 0

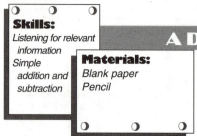

Adam's Apples

I am going to read a story about apples. At the end of the story I will ask you how many apples Adam has. I will repeat the story for you when I have finished it the first time. Begin by writing your name in the top right corner of your page.

Adam overslept and missed his breakfast. He had just enough time to get dressed and grab his lunch before he started his walk to school.

"I sure am hungry," Adam thought as he walked through the park. "I think I'll take a peek to see what's in my lunch box." Great news! Adam's mom had packed a sandwich, some carrot sticks and 2 apples. "This is my lucky day!" thought Adam as he munched on 1 apple.

As he turned down Main Street, Adam met Sam the grocer as he was putting out the day's fresh fruit. "Hey, Adam," Sam called. "Let me give you some apples. You can take these to school and share them with your friends. He handed Adam 4 shiny red apples. Adam put them in his lunch box.

At school Adam decided to give 1 apple to his teacher. He gave another 1 to his best friend, Ryan. He ate 1 for himself at lunch.

How many apples did Adam have left? I will read the story once more. If you like, you may make marks on your paper and cross them out to help keep track of the apples. (Repeat story.) Now I want you to write down the number of apples Adam had at the end of the story. Make your number large and circle it. Then draw that many apples on your page.

Welcome to my apple!

Welcome

Skills:
Finding sums of 10

Materials:
Blank paper
Pencil

Ten Sums

1. Draw a line in the middle of your paper from the top to the bottom of the page.

2. On the left-hand side of your page write these numbers in a column going down: 7, 3, 2, 9, 6, 1, 4, 10, 5, 8, 0

3. On the right-hand side of your page write these numbers in a column going down: 6, 1, 0, 4, 7, 9, 2, 8, 3, 10, 5

4. Now draw a line from the first number on the left to the number on the right that can be added to it to make 10.

5. Continue drawing lines from numbers on the left to the numbers on the right that will connect pairs that add up to 10.

6. Write your name on the bottom of the page.

Skills:
Mental computations
Addition with addends
1-9

Materials:
Lined paper
Pencil

Score More

Write your name in the top left corner of your paper. Number your paper from 1 to 10. For each number, I will read two math problems. Write down just the answer to the problem that has the highest sum. For example, if I ask you, "Which is more, 1 + 1 or 5 + 5?" you would simply write down 10, the highest sum.

1. Which is more, 8 + 5 or 7 + 9?
2. Which is more, 6 + 8 or 9 + 3?
3. Which is more, 8 + 8 or 9 + 6?
4. Which is more, 4 + 9 or 5 + 6?
5. Which is more, 6 + 7 or 9 + 5?
6. Which is more, 3 + 8 or 5 + 7?
7. Which is more, 7 + 7 or 5 + 8?
8. Which is more, 6 + 6 or 9 + 4?
9. Which is more, 7 + 8 or 9 + 9?
10. Which is more, 4 + 8 or 7 + 6?

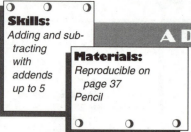

Skills:
Adding and subtracting with addends up to 5

Materials:
Reproducible on page 37
Pencil

ADDITION AND SUBTRACTION

Add the Signs

1. Put your name in the top right corner of your page.

2. In row A, place an addition sign in each problem.
   Then write the answers for row A.

3. In row B, place a subtraction sign in each problem.
   Write the answers for row B.

4. In row C, we will make a pattern of addition and subtraction signs. In the first problem, write an addition sign. In the second problem, write a subtraction sign. In the third problem, write an addition sign. Finish the pattern. Now write the answers to all the problems in row C.

5. Circle all the problems with an answer of 1.

6. Finally, underline all the problems with an answer of 2.

Add the Signs

Reproducible for use with page 36.

A.
3	4	5	3	4	4
1	3	1	0	4	2

B.
5	3	5	4	5	2
0	2	4	1	3	1

C.
1	3	5	4	2	0
1	3	5	4	2	0

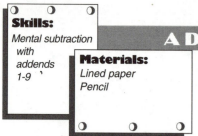

Skills:
Mental subtraction
with
addends
1-9

Materials:
Lined paper
Pencil

Speedy Subtraction

First write your name in the top left corner of your page. Number your paper from 1 to 24. I will read you 24 subtraction problems, and I want you to write the answer to each on the corresponding line on your paper. I will move rather quickly, so listen closely and get ready to THINK! (Problems and speed can vary with abilities of your group.)

1. 10 - 1	9. 15 - 7	17. 17 - 9
2. 12 - 3	10. 16 - 9	18. 10 - 7
3. 9 - 6	11. 14 - 7	19. 16 - 8
4. 13 - 5	12. 11 - 4	20. 14 - 5
5. 12 - 7	13. 13 - 9	21. 11 - 3
6. 14 - 8	14. 15 - 6	22. 16 - 7
7. 10 - 6	15. 12 - 6	23. 15 - 8
8. 11 - 5	16. 18 - 9	24. 10 - 2

Ups and Downs

Skills:
Mental subtraction

Materials:
Lined paper
Pencil

Number your paper from 1 to 10. I will read 10 little stories. After each one, you will need to write down either the word *up* or *down*, followed by a number. (The teacher may or may not wish to require labels on numbers.)

1. On Monday, the temperature outside was 15 degrees. On Tuesday, it was 8 degrees. Did the temperature go up or down? By how much?

2. Last week 2 dinners at Chef Jeff's cost $10. This week they cost $12. Did the price go up or down? By how much?

3. Last year my antique dish was worth $80. Now it is worth $90. Did the value of my dish go up or down? By how much?

4. Last year there were 18 students in second grade. This year there are 11. Did the number of students go up or down? By how much?

5. Last Saturday, Ryan delivered 50 newspapers. This Saturday he delivered 55 newspapers. Did the number of papers Ryan delivered go up or down? By how much?

6. The bag of marbles I bought last week contained 12 marbles. The bag I bought today contains 8 marbles. Did the number of marbles go up or down? By how much?

7. Last Sunday I had 20 people over for dinner. This Sunday I had 24. Did the number of people go up or down? By how much?

8. A flock of 40 birds flew over my house an hour ago. Just now another flock of 30 birds flew over. Did the number of birds go up or down? By how much?

9. The number of stories for this page started at 10. Now the number is at 1. Did the number of stories go up or down? By how much?

10. The first quilt I made had 15 squares. My second quilt has 18 squares. Did the number of squares go up or down? By how much?

11. Write your name next to your answer on line 1.

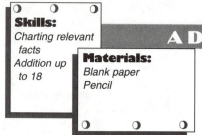

Skills:
Charting relevant facts
Addition up to 18

Materials:
Blank paper
Pencil

A D D I T I O N   A N D   S U B T R A C T I O N

Scoreboard

In this lesson I will read you information about a baseball game. At the end I will ask you how many hits each team had, how many runs each team had, and which team won the game. I will give you all the information you need, so listen carefully. The two teams are the Hawks and the Caps. They will play 7 innings. Take a few minutes now to set up a chart that will help you keep track of important information. (At the teacher's discretion, a sample chart could be drawn on the board for students to copy.)

It could look like this:

Hawks

Inning	1	2	3	4	5	6	7	Total
Hits								
Runs								

Caps

Inning	1	2	3	4	5	6	7	Total
Hits								
Runs								

Story:

In the first inning the Hawks had no hits and no runs. The Caps had 3 hits and 1 run. In the second inning the Hawks had 2 hits but still no runs. The Caps had 2 more hits but no runs. In the third inning, the Hawks broke loose with 7 hits and 3 runs. The Caps came back with 2 hits and 1 run. In the fourth inning both teams had no hits and no runs. In the fifth inning the Hawks had 4 hits and 2 runs. The Caps had 2 hits and 1 run. The sixth inning was an exact repeat of the fifth inning. In the seventh inning, the Hawks had 1 hit but no runs. The Caps slugged out 6 hits and 4 runs.

Now under your chart write the name of the winning team and circle it. Put the total number of *runs* they had next to it.

Write the name of the team with the most *hits* and underline it. Write the number of hits next to the team name. Write your name under the team names.

Skills:
Two-digit addition and subtraction without regrouping

Materials:
Lined paper
Pencil

Oops!

Prince Addley is having trouble with his royal math lesson today. He has made a lot of mistakes which you need to find. I will read you 3 rows of math problems. There will be 4 problems going across your paper in each row. Copy each problem and answer that I read. (Show students on the chalkboard, if necessary, how to write problems vertically.)

Read these problems:

First row:

24	15	21	84
+ 42	+ 83	+ 34	+ 14
66	97	45	98

Second row:

78	37	96	16
− 20	+ 42	− 34	+ 63
48	49	51	78

Third row:

89	76	50	64
− 54	− 31	− 20	− 31
45	44	30	33

Now check over Prince Addley's work. Circle any addition problems he missed. Underline any subtraction problems he missed. Now be extra helpful and write the correct answer under each missed problem. Finally, write your name on the top left corner.

I'm having trouble with my royal math.

I'll help you!

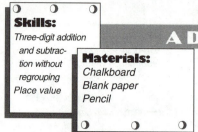

Skills:
Three-digit addition and subtraction without regrouping
Place value

Materials:
Chalkboard
Blank paper
Pencil

ADDITION AND SUBTRACTION

Chalkboard Challenge

Before the lesson, write these 10 rows of numbers on the chalkboard.

1.	735	121	649	6.	268	413	83
2.	530	496	367	7.	193	222	74
3.	675	809	432	8.	136	600	249
4.	194	73	126	9.	25	910	31
5.	98	801	795	10.	36	102	521

You need to number your paper from 1 to 10. Leave enough space between numbers to write addition and subtraction problems, along with their answers. Put your name in the upper right corner of your page. Now look at the numbers on the board. I will give you a set of directions for each line. You will write the correct problem and the answer by the same number on your paper.

1. For row 1, subtract the lowest number from the highest number.

2. For row 2, add the lowest number to the highest number.

3. For row 3, add the lowest number to itself.

4. For row 4, subtract the lowest number from the highest number.

5. For row 5, copy the highest number. Write a new number by reversing its digits. Add these numbers together.

6. For row 6, add the highest number to itself.

7. For row 7, add the lowest number to the highest number.

8. For row 8, copy the lowest number. Write a new number by reversing its digits. Add these numbers together.

9. For rows 9 and 10, add all three numbers together.

Three-Digit Doodles

Skills:
*Addition and subtraction
with regrouping
Estimation*

Materials:
*Reproducible on
page 44*

1. Write your name in the top right corner.

2. In row A, circle the problem that you think will have the lowest answer.

3. Solve the problems in row A. If you circled the right answer, put a star under your name.

4. In row B, circle the problem that you think will have the highest answer.

5. Next, write the answer to every problem in row B. If you circled the problem with the highest answer, put a happy face under your name.

6. Now look at the subtraction problems in row C. Circle the problem you think will have the lowest answer.

7. Now solve the problems in row C. If you circled the right problem, write *OK* under your name.

8. Look at all the answers on your paper. Underline all the answers that read the same backward and forward.

9. Under row C, start a row D. In this new row, try to write an addition problem where the answer will be 999.

10. Also in row D, try to write a subtraction problem where the answer will be 111.

Three-Digit Doodles

Reproducible for use with page 43.

A.
$$\begin{array}{r} 396 \\ + 412 \\ \hline \end{array}$$
$$\begin{array}{r} 708 \\ + 133 \\ \hline \end{array}$$
$$\begin{array}{r} 614 \\ + 416 \\ \hline \end{array}$$
$$\begin{array}{r} 324 \\ + 140 \\ \hline \end{array}$$

B.
$$\begin{array}{r} 168 \\ + 591 \\ \hline \end{array}$$
$$\begin{array}{r} 890 \\ + 346 \\ \hline \end{array}$$
$$\begin{array}{r} 705 \\ + 434 \\ \hline \end{array}$$
$$\begin{array}{r} 281 \\ + 243 \\ \hline \end{array}$$

C.
$$\begin{array}{r} 429 \\ - 36 \\ \hline \end{array}$$
$$\begin{array}{r} 652 \\ - 507 \\ \hline \end{array}$$
$$\begin{array}{r} 735 \\ - 180 \\ \hline \end{array}$$
$$\begin{array}{r} 267 \\ - 35 \\ \hline \end{array}$$

Multiplication and Division

Materials:
Reproducible on page 46
Pencil

1. Write your name above box A.

2. Draw 2 children in box A. Decide how to divide the cookies fairly between the 2 children. Draw a circle around a set for each child. Then draw a line from each child to his set of cookies.

3. Two friends each bought 3 balloons. How many balloons did they buy in all? Write your answer in the blank by letter *B*.

4. Look at part C. Write in a multiplication sign next to the 4 on the first blank. In the second blank write the number you would multiply by 4 to reach an answer of 12. Finish the other blanks in the same way.

5. Look at part D. Here you see prices of parts at a hardware store. Listen to the items Sue is buying. Figure out how much she will spend. Sue needs 4 nails plus 1 bolt. Write how much she will spend next to her name. Tom will buy 2 nuts, 2 bolts and 2 nails. How much will Tom spend? Write your answer next to Tom's name.

6. Look at the boxes in part E. Put an *X* on the answer to 3 x 6. Circle the answer to 4 x 7.

Multiplication and Division

A.

B. _____

C. 4 __ _____ = 12   5 __ _____ = 15   7 __ _____ = 14

D. Hardware prices: nails–2¢, nuts–3¢, bolts–5¢

Sue _____ Tom _____

E.

16	17	18	19	20
26	27	28	29	30

Pet Pals

Skills:
Simple division

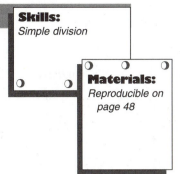

Materials:
Reproducible on page 48

Use as a Warm-Up for Part 4.

1. Find the box on your paper that contains bones. Draw 2 dogs inside this box.

2. Now decide how to divide the bones fairly between the 2 dogs. Draw a circle around a set of bones for each dog. Then draw a line from each dog to his set of bones. Be sure each has the same amount.

3. Find the box with the pieces of cheese. Draw 3 mice inside this box.

4. Now decide how to divide the cheese evenly among the 3 mice. Draw a circle around a set of cheese pieces for each mouse.
Then draw a line to connect each mouse to his cheese.

5. Find the box with the balls. Draw 4 kittens inside the box.

6. Now decide how to divide the balls evenly among the 4 kittens.
Draw a ring around a set of balls for each kitten.
Then draw a line to connect each set of balls with a kitten.

7. Find the box with the 2 bird feeders. Draw 4 birds inside the box.

8. Now decide how the birds can share the feeders evenly. Draw a line from each bird to a feeder so that each feeder is feeding the same number of birds.

9. Write your name at the bottom of the page.

Pet Pals

Reproducible for use with page 47.

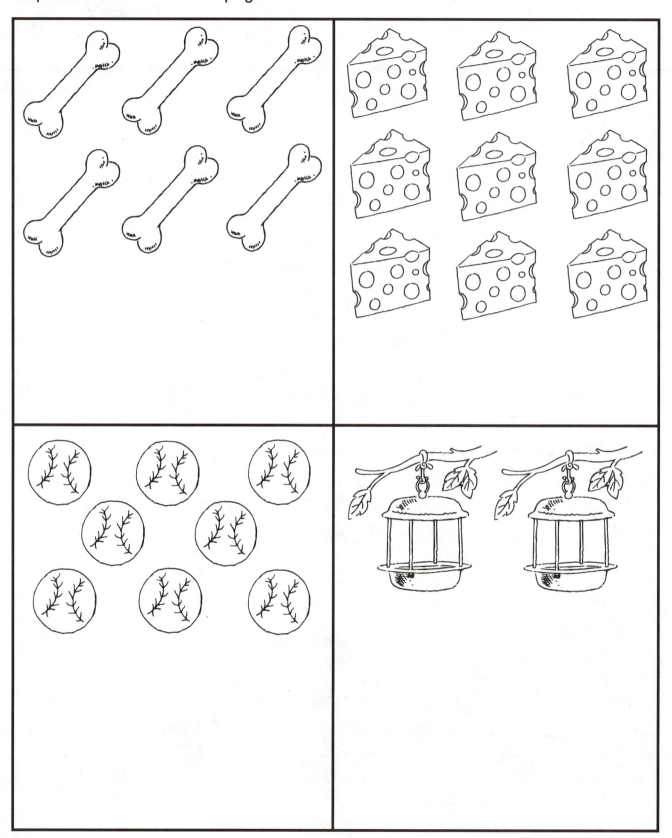

Multiple Stories

Skills:
One-digit multipliers

Materials:
Lined paper
Pencil

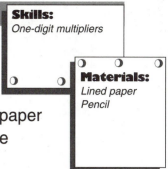

Write your name in the top left corner of your paper. Number your paper from 1 to 9. For each number, I will read you a little story. Write the answer to each story beside each number.

1. Two friends each bought 2 balloons at the circus. How many balloons did they buy in all?

2. A set of triplets decided to go to the circus. Each one wanted her hair braided into 2 pigtails. How many pigtails did their mom fix in all?

3. Four elephants each got fancy new tassels to put on all 4 of their feet. How many tassels were there in all?

4. A pair of horses needed all new horseshoes before they performed at the circus. How many shoes did their trainer have to change in all?

5. The ringmaster at the three-ring circus introduced 3 poodles in the first ring, 3 elephants in the second ring and 3 lions in the third ring. How many animals were performing altogether?

6. A boy was selling bags of peanuts in the bleachers. In each bag there were 5 peanut shells, and there were 2 nuts inside each shell. How many separate nuts were there in each bag?

7. There was also a lady in the bleachers selling cotton candy for $1 a package. One father bought 3 packages for his children. How many dollars did he owe the lady for the candy?

8. Three acrobats needed new pairs of gloves to match their costumes. How many separate gloves did the seamstress need to sew?

9. The animals were loaded into cages and put on trailers right after the circus. The lions were put on 3 different trailers, each with 4 tires. The driver wanted to check the air on all the tires hauling the lions. How many tires did he have to check?

Skills:
Multiplication through 5 x 5 with missing factors

Materials:
Lined paper
Pencil

MULTIPLICATION AND DIVISION

Line Up

1. Write your name in the top right corner of your paper.

2. Divide your paper into 3 columns by drawing 2 lines from the top to the bottom of your paper.

3. Next you will write numbers in the first column. Start at the top and write one number on each line. These are the numbers to write in the first column in order: 4, 1, 5, 2, 3, 4, 5, 3, 2, 1, 4, 5.

4. Next to each number you just wrote, write in a multiplication sign.

5. Leave the second column blank for now.

6. Next you'll write numbers in the third column. Write them, one on each line, under each other so they line up with the numbers you wrote in the first column. Here are the numbers to write in the third column in order: 8, 5, 15, 6, 12, 16, 10, 9, 4, 0, 20, 25.

7. Now write the number in the second column that will make a correct multiplication problem. After the number write an equals sign. For example, on your first line you will need to write "2 =" because 4 x 2 = 8.

8. Now draw a ring around each problem that has 2 matching factors, such as 1 x 1. You should have circled 4 math problems.

Optional Variation:

If desired, the teacher could "flip" this lesson around so that the students are writing obvious division problems. They could be instructed to put the third column numbers in the first column, followed by division signs. Then the numbers that were originally to be placed in the first column could go in the second column. Finally, the students would then need to complete the problems by writing the answers in the last column. Also, numbers can be changed to form more difficult problems as students' abilities increase.

Candy Shop

Skills:
Multiplication through
5 x 5 with addition

Materials:
Lined paper
Pencil

Several friends bought some candy. Listen carefully to this information so you can tell how much money each person spent. You will want to write down some of the information I am giving you. First you need to know the price of different kinds of candy.

Suckers are 5 cents each. Gum is 3 cents a piece. Jelly beans are 2 cents each.

(Repeat prices or write them on the chalkboard.) Now figure out how much each child spent on candy. Number your paper from 1 to 10. On each line write the child's name (don't worry about spelling) and the price he paid.

1. Tasha bought 3 pieces of gum. By number 1 write her name and the price she paid. (Repeat this part of the directions as necessary throughout the lesson.)

2. Gary bought 3 jelly beans and 1 sucker.

3. Ann bought 1 sucker, 1 piece of gum and 1 jelly bean.

4. Lee bought 5 suckers.

5. Amy bought 4 jelly beans plus 1 sucker.

6. Omar bought 3 pieces of gum plus 1 jelly bean.

7. Ed bought 2 pieces of each kind of candy.

8. Jill bought 3 suckers and 1 jelly bean.

9. Rob bought 4 pieces of gum and 1 sucker.

10. Circle the name of the person who spent the most.

11. Underline the name of the person who spent the least.

12. Write your name on the top of your page.

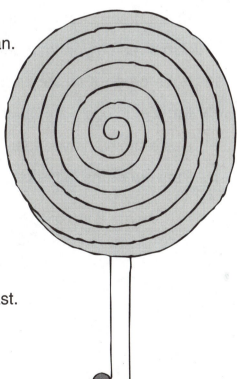

Skills:
Multiplication through 7 x 7

Materials:
Reproducible on page 15 (Bottom half of chart can be omitted or covered.) Crayons: red, yellow, blue, green, black, brown

MULTIPLICATION AND DIVISION

Colored Products

1. With a black crayon, color the square that has the answer to 2 x 7.

2. Use a red crayon to color the square that has the answer to 4 x 6.

3. Use a yellow crayon to color the square that has the answer to 7 x 7.

4. Use a green crayon to circle the answer to 5 x 7.

5. Use a blue crayon to underline the answer to 6 x 6.

6. Put a brown *X* on the answer to 4 x 7.

7. Put a red *X* on the answer to 4 x 4.

8. Put a black circle around the answer to 3 x 7.

9. Put a yellow circle around the answer to 6 x 5.

10. Use a green crayon to underline the answer to 3 x 6.

11. Use a red crayon to underline the answer to 4 x 5.

12. Put a green *X* on the answer to 3 x 4.

13. Put a blue circle around the answer to 6 x 7.

14. Use a brown crayon to underline the answer to 2 x 6.

15. Put your name in the upper right-hand corner.

Materials:
Reproducible on page 54
Pencil
Ruler

Time, Money and Measurement

1. On clock A, add these numbers where they belong:
   1, 2, 4, 5, 7, 8, 10, 11. Add an hour hand and a minute hand.
   Write your name under clock A.

2. Look at the 2 clocks by letter *B*. Underline the clock that reads
   2 o'clock.

3. Look at clock C. If Mr. Smith leaves for the beach at this time and drives
   for 2$\frac{1}{2}$ hours, what time will he arrive at the beach? Write your answer in digital
   form under clock C.

4. In box D, circle enough coins to make 7 cents.

5. In box E, underline the amount of money Jane would have if she started with
   10 cents and spent 4 cents.

6. How much money would you have if you found these coins: 2 dimes, 1 nickel
   and 3 pennies? Write your answer by letter *F*.

7. Jose has 2 quarters and 2 dimes. Can he buy a treat that costs 75 cents?
   Write *yes* or *no* next to letter *G*.

8. Look at the lines by letter *H*. Circle the one that is 2 inches long.

9. Near the top of the space marked I, draw a horizontal line that is 8 cm long.

10. Under that line, draw a rectangle that is 6 cm wide and 4 cm high. Put an *X*
    inside the rectangle on the spot that is 1 cm above the bottom of the rectangle
    and 1 cm away from the left-hand side of the rectangle.

Time, Money, and Measurement

A.

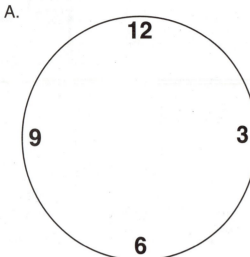

B.

C.

D.

E.

F. _____

G. _____

H. _____ _____ _____

I.

Clocks, Coins and Rulers

Materials:
Classroom clocks
Large numbered
 pieces of paper or
 cardboard
Sticks
Coins
Rulers

Use as a Warm-Up for Part 5.

Time:

1. Using classroom clocks with movable arms, have students practice setting the hands for times you give them orally. Start with hours, then half hours.

2. If space allows, make your own classroom clock. Place 12 students in a large circle with each one holding a large piece of paper with a number from 1 to 12. The other students can hold long sticks, yardsticks or cardboard pointers for the "hands" of the clock and take turns making the classroom clock read different times.

3. Using the clock on the wall, throughout the day do some oral clock "math." Ask questions such as, "If it's 1 o'clock now, what time will it be in 1 hour?" "2 hours?" "What time was it 1 hour ago?" "3 hours ago?"

Money:

1. Go over values of different coins. Practice finding coin sums using play or real coins. Do a lot of oral work; for example, "Show me 2 coins that make 6 cents." "Show me 3 coins that make 25 cents." "How much is 1 nickel, 1 dime and 2 pennies?"

2. Have a classroom store. Let students practice buying, selling and making change with play money for small classroom supplies, grocery items, etc.

Measurement:

1. Hold up two or three objects. Ask which is longer, shorter.

2. Give students rulers that measure in inches. Ask them to find an item on or near their desk that is 2 inches long, 5 inches long, etc. Repeat using centimeters.

Skills:
Drawing a clock

Materials:
Blank paper
Pencil

TIME, MONEY AND MEASUREMENT

Time to Draw

(Note: Teacher need not tell students at the beginning of the lesson that they are drawing a clock.)

1. Draw a large circle in the center of your paper.

2. Draw a square around the outside of your circle. Write your name under the square.

3. Now shade in the "frame," the area between the circle and the square.

4. Write the number 12 inside the circle, exactly at the top.

5. At the very bottom of the inside of the circle, write the number 6.

6. Halfway between the 12 and 6 on the *right* side of the circle, write the number 3 inside the circle.

7. Halfway between the 6 and the 12 on the *left*, write the number 9 inside the circle.

8. Now in the space between the 12 and 3, write the numbers 1 and 2 in order.

9. Fill in these numbers in order around the rest of the circle:
   4, 5, 7, 8, 10 and 11.

10. Put a dot in the middle of the circle. Make a short arrow from the dot pointing to the 3. Make a longer arrow from the dot pointing to the 12.

Skills:
Telling time on the hour

Materials:
Reproducible on page 58
Crayons: red, blue, yellow, green

Hour Time

1. Find the clock that says 7 o'clock. Color it yellow.

2. Find the clock that says 3 o'clock. Color it blue.

3. Find the clock that says 4 o'clock. Write your name above it.

4. Find the clock that says 12 o'clock. Underline it.

5. Find the clock that says 2 o'clock. Color it green.

6. Find the clock that says 10 o'clock. Color it red.

7. Circle the clock that says 6 o'clock.

8. In the bottom row, make the first clock read 11 o'clock.
   Make the second clock read 5 o'clock.
   Make the third clock read 1 o'clock.

RRRRRRRIIIIIINNNGGG

UP 'N' AT 'EM!

Clocks

Reproducible for use with pages 57 and 59.

A.

B.

C.

D.

E.

F.

G.

H.

I.

J.

K.

L.

Time to Add

Skills:
Adding and subtracting with time (hours and half hours)

Materials:
Reproducible on page 58

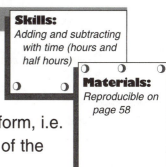

Instruct students to write their answers on the worksheet in digital form, i.e. 9:00 for 9 o'clock. Also instruct them to put their names at the top of the page.

1. Look at clock D. If Mr. Smith leaves for work at this time and drives for 1½ hours, what time will he arrive at work? Write your answer under clock D.

2. Look at clock H. If Baby Ali wakes up from her nap at this time after sleeping for 2 hours, what time did she fall asleep? Write your answer under clock H.

3. Look at clock I. If this is the time school starts, and school lasts for 7 hours, what time does school end? Write your answer under clock I.

4. Look at clock C. If Mrs. Jones took a 4½-hour airplane flight and arrived at this time, what time did she leave? Write your answer under clock C.

5. Look at clock G. If Tom starts some homemade soup at this time and it needs to simmer for 2½ hours, at what time will the soup be done? Write your answer under clock G.

6. Look at clock F. If Pam starts painting at this time, paints for 4 hours, takes a break for 1 hour and paints for 2 more hours, what time will it be when she finishes? Write your answer under clock F.

7. Look at clock B. If Billy goes to bed at this time and sleeps for 9½ hours, what time does he get up? Write your answer under clock B.

8. Look at clock J. Draw hands on it to show what time it would be if Jack started work at 7:30 and worked for 8½ hours?

9. Now go to clock K. Draw hands on it to show what time the Fisher family should leave for their vacation. They want to arrive at 6:00 p.m., and they have a 10-hour drive.

10. On clock L draw the time Scott got home last Saturday. He left at 3:00, drove for ½ an hour, went to a movie for 2 hours, went to a restaurant for 1 hour and drove back home for ½ an hour.

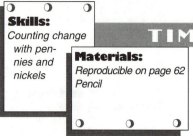

Skills:
Counting change with pennies and nickels

Materials:
*Reproducible on page 62
Pencil*

Coin Count

1. Write your name at the top of your paper.

2. In row A, circle enough pennies to make 5 cents.

3. In row B, circle enough pennies to make 3 cents.

4. In row C, circle enough pennies to make 7 cents.

5. In row D, circle enough pennies to make 8 cents.

6. In row E, notice that we now have a nickel along with some pennies. Circle the amount of coins that will make 6 cents.

7. In row F, circle enough coins to make 8 cents.

8. In row G, circle enough coins to make 4 cents.

9. In row H, circle enough coins to make 9 cents.

Coin Math

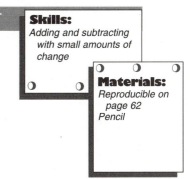

Skills:
Adding and subtracting with small amounts of change

Materials:
Reproducible on page 62
Pencil

1. Write your name in the top right corner of your page.

2. In row A, circle the number of coins Keith has if he started with 10 cents and spent 7 cents.

3. In row B, underline the amount of money Li-An has if she started with 8 cents and gave away 4 cents.

4. In row C, circle the amount of money Randy has if he started with 4 cents and found 3 cents more.

5. In row D, underline the amount of money Teri has when she started with 10 cents and spent 5 cents.

6. In row E, circle the amount of money Carlos has when he started with 6 cents and was given 2 cents.

7. In row F, circle the amount of money Dale has when he started with 3 cents and earned 7 cents more.

8. In row G, underline the amount of money Gina has when she started with 7 cents and found 2 cents more.

9. Count the money in row H. Write the total amount at the bottom of the page.

Coins

Reproducible for use with pages 60 and 61.

A.

B.

C.

D.

E.

F.

G.

H.

Betsy's Birthday

Skills:
Listening for details
Adding with pennies,
nickels and
dimes

Materials:
Blank paper
Pencil

I'm going to read you a story called "Betsy's Birthday." When I have finished the story, I will ask you to write down how much money Betsy had at the end of the story. You may want to take notes on your paper as I read to you.

Story:

It was Betsy's seventh birthday. She was so excited that she woke up very early in the morning. The rest of her family was still asleep, but Betsy got up anyway. On the kitchen table she found a note that said: "Dear Betsy, We thought you might be up early, so we made a surprise for you. It's a treasure hunt! If you can guess our secret hiding places you will find seven coins, each from the year you were born. Good luck! Love, Mom and Dad."

Betsy searched high and low. Finally she found a dime under a coaster. There was a nickel in the magazine rack. After a little more looking she spotted a penny in the plant dish and a dime behind the clock. Under the sofa cushion Betsy found a nickel. After a lot more looking, she came across another nickel under the VCR. She counted six coins. Where was number seven? She finally found it–a penny under the doormat.

Just then Betsy's parents walked into the room. "Happy Birthday, Betsy!" they said.

Now write down how much money Betsy found altogether. Write your name under your answer.

Here are two tough bonus questions you may try to answer also.

1. Where was the first coin hidden that Betsy found?
2. Where was the last coin hidden that she found?

Skills:
Comparing coin sums with pennies, nickels, dimes and quarters

Materials:
Blank paper
Pencil

TIME, MONEY AND MEASUREMENT

Coin Comparison

Divide your paper into 2 columns by drawing a line from top to bottom. In the left-hand column, first write your name. Then number from 1 to 10. The right-hand column will be your work space. I will read you 10 short story problems, and at the end of each one I will ask you a question. Write the answer beside each number.

1. Joy has 3 quarters. Does she have enough money to buy a ring that costs 60 cents?

2. Phil has 2 dimes and 2 nickels. Does he have enough money to give his brother 15 cents and keep 15 cents for himself?

3. Suzanne has 4 nickels and 5 pennies. Can she buy a 30-cent candy bar?

4. Alex has 2 quarters and 2 dimes. Can he buy a ruler that costs 65 cents?

5. Pam has 1 quarter, 1 dime and 1 nickel. How much money does she have in all?

6. Melissa has 1 quarter, 2 dimes and 4 pennies. How much money does she have in all?

7. Which boy, Joe or Carlos, has the most money? Joe has 2 quarters and Carlos has 3 dimes plus 5 nickels. Write *J* for *Joe* or *C* for *Carlos*.

8. Which girl, Beth or Sally, has the least money? Beth has 1 nickel and 7 pennies. Sally has 1 dime and 3 pennies. Write *B* for *Beth* or *S* for *Sally*.

9. Jill spent 2 dimes at the candy store. Carrie spent 3 nickels and 3 pennies. Which girl spent the most on the candy? Write *J* for *Jill* or *C* for *Carrie*.

10. Bryan spent 2 quarters and 2 nickels on fishing bait. Ryan spent 3 dimes and 5 nickels. Which boy spent the most on bait? Write *B* for *Bryan* or *R* for *Ryan*.

Skills:
Measuring in inches

Materials:
Reproducible on
page 66
Crayons: blue,
brown, yellow
Ruler

Inchworms

1. Find the worm that is 3 inches long. Write your name under that worm.

2. Find the worm that is only 1 inch long. Put an *X* on it.

3. Find the worm that is 5 inches long. Color it brown.

4. Find the worm that is 4 inches long. Color it yellow.

5. Find the worm that is 2 inches long. Underline it.

6. Find the worm that is 7 inches long. Color it blue.

7. Find the worm that is 6 inches long. Circle it.

Skills:
Measuring in
centimeters

Materials:
Blank paper
Ruler marked in
centimeters
Pencil

Centimeter Draw

1. Divide your paper in half by drawing a line from the left side to the right side across the middle of your page.

2. Draw a horizontal line near the top of your paper that is 12 centimeters long. Put a letter *A* by it.

3. Under line A, draw another horizontal line that is 7 centimeters long. Put a letter *B* by it.

4. Under line B, draw a line that is 5 centimeters long. Label it with letter *C*.

5. Under line C, draw a line that is 10 centimeters long. Label it with a letter *D*.

6. Draw a box in the bottom half of your paper that is 15 centimeters wide and 10 centimeters high.

7. Inside the box, draw a square that is 6 centimeters long on each side. Write your name in the square.

Inchworms

Reproducible for use with page 65.

Skills:
Measuring in inches

Materials:
Blank paper
Ruler (inches)
Pencil

X Marks the Spot

For this lesson, we are going on a treasure hunt. See if you can find the spot where the treasure is buried.

A. First write your name in the upper right corner of your paper.

B. Now find the lower left corner of your paper. From this corner, measure 2 inches straight up. Make a small dot there.

C. From your dot measure 3 inches directly to the right. Make a dot at that place and label it with a capital *A*.

D. Measure 2 inches straight up from point A. Make another dot and label it with a capital *B*.

E. Now measure 4 inches to the right of B. Make a dot and label it with a capital *C*.

F. Next measure 3 inches below C. Make and label it with a capital *D*.

G. Now use your ruler to draw a straight line connecting A and C.

H. Make another straight line connecting B and D.

I. Put a large dark *X* on the place where your two lines meet.
That *X* marks the spot for buried treasure!

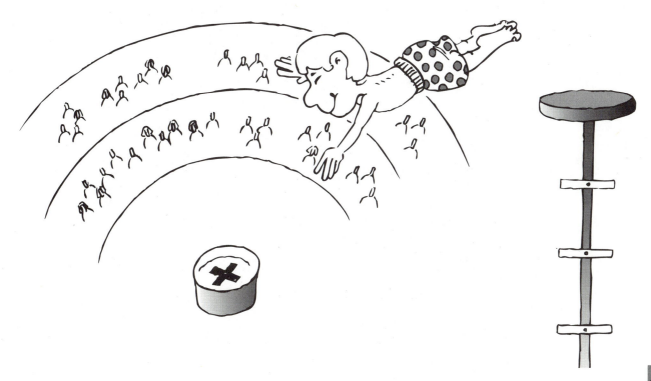

Materials:
*Reproducible on page 69
Pencil*

Fractions

1. Draw a square in space A. Shade in ¹⁄₂ of the square with your pencil. Write your name under the square.

2. In space B, draw 3 balls. Shade ¹⁄₃ of the balls with your pencil.

3. Look at part C. Find the rectangle that's divided into fifths. Color in ²⁄₅ of the rectangle.

4. Find the circle in part C that's divided into fourths. Color in ³⁄₄ of the circle.

5. Find 2 shapes in part C that are divided into thirds. Underline both shapes.

6. Look at the faces in part D. Give ⁴⁄₆ (²⁄₃) of the faces smiles. Give ²⁄₆ (¹⁄₃) of the faces frowns.

7. Give ¹⁄₆ of the faces a large nose. Give ⁵⁄₆ of the faces small noses.

8. Give ²⁄₆ (¹⁄₃) of the faces curly hair.

9. Put hats on ³⁄₆ (¹⁄₂) of the faces.

10. Add ears to ⁵⁄₆ of the faces.

Fractions

A.

B.

C.

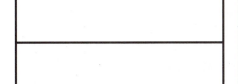  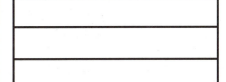

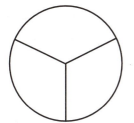 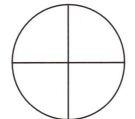 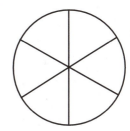

D.

Fraction Action

Use as a Warm-Up for Part 6.

1. Hold up both of your hands. Put $\frac{1}{2}$ of your hands behind your back.

2. Hold up all five fingers on one hand. Put $\frac{1}{5}$ of your fingers down.
   Put $\frac{4}{5}$ of your fingers down. Put $\frac{2}{5}$ of your fingers down. Put $\frac{5}{5}$ of your fingers down.

3. Bring three children to the front of the room. Depending on the children selected, ask questions such as these:

   How many of the children are girls (boys)?

   How many of the children have brown (blonde, black, red) hair?

   How many of the children are wearing red (brown, blue, green, etc.)?

   Ask the students to respond with answers expressed as fractions, such as "two-thirds of the children are girls."

4. Repeat number three above with larger groups of students using a variety of questions.

5. For older students who may be able to work with fractions in lowest terms, you could work with four children, for example, where 2 are boys and 2 are girls. Such students may be able to tell you that $\frac{2}{4}$ of the children are girls, and also that $\frac{1}{2}$ of the children are girls.

6. You may also try some chalkboard activities. Ask several students to come to the board and draw a pie cut in 6 pieces. Ask them to shade in $\frac{1}{6}$ or $\frac{5}{6}$ of the pie. Repeat with other students using different shapes and fractions.

Fraction Draw

Skills:
Drawing fractions with halves, thirds and fourths

Materials:
Blank paper
Pencil

1. Fold your paper so that the top edge touches the bottom edge. Then fold the left edge over to the right edge. Crease both folds and open your paper. You should now have 4 equal rectangles.

2. In the top left rectangle, draw a large circle. Shade in 1/2 of the circle lightly with your pencil. Write your name in the blank half of the circle.

3. In the bottom left rectangle, draw 3 hearts. Shade 2/3 of the hearts with your pencil.

4. In the top right rectangle, draw 4 candy canes. Draw a ring around 3/4 of the candy canes.

5. In the bottom rectangle of your paper, draw a large square. Divide it into 4 equal parts. Shade 1/4 of the square with your pencil.

Fractured Shapes

Skills:
Identifying fractional parts

Materials:
Reproducible on page 72
Pencil or crayon

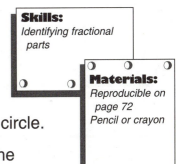

1. Find the circle that is divided into 2 parts. Shade in 1/2 of the circle.

2. Find the rectangle that is divided into thirds. Shade in 2/3 of the rectangle.

3. Find the 2 squares that are divided into fourths. Circle them.

4. Find the rectangle divided into sevenths. Color in 5/7 of the rectangle.

5. Find the circle that is divided into thirds. Write your name above it.

6. Put an *X* above every shape that is divided into fourths. Shade in 1/4 of each of these objects.

F.actured Shapes

Reproducible for use with page 71.

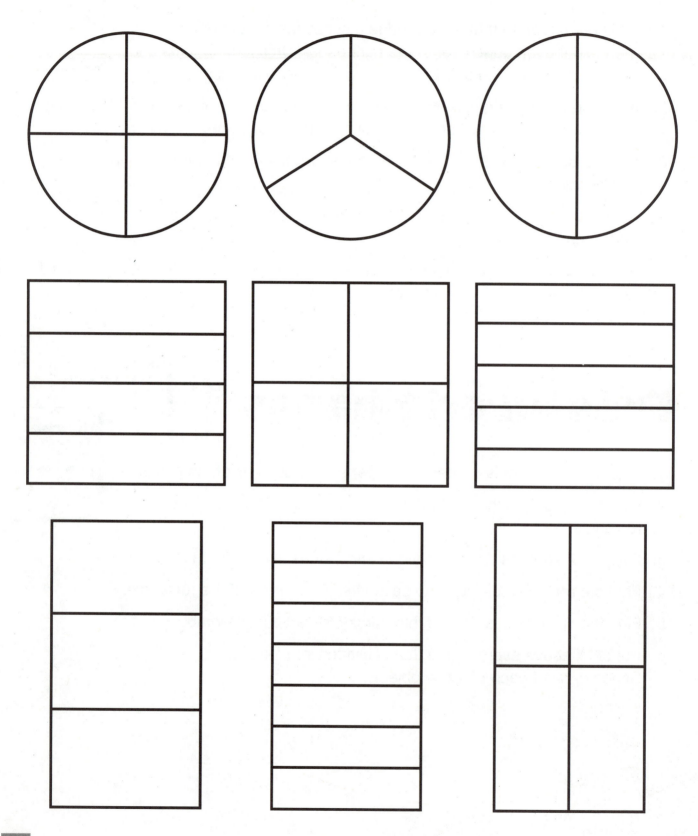

Home Improvements

Skills:
Identifying fractional parts

Materials:
Reproducible on page 74
Crayons: red, green
Pencil

(For advanced students you could read the reduced fraction in ( ) instead of the first fraction given.)

1. Put chimneys on $6/12$ ($1/2$) of the houses.

2. Put a front door on $9/12$ ($3/4$) of the houses.

3. Draw a small bush on the right side of $4/12$ ($1/3$) of the houses.

4. Give $5/12$ of the houses two windows.

5. Give $3/12$ ($1/4$) of the houses four windows.

6. Give $4/12$ ($1/3$) of the houses one window.

7. Draw a small tree on the left side of $2/12$ ($1/6$) of the houses.

8. Color $6/12$ ($1/2$) of the roofs green.

9. Color $4/12$ ($1/3$) of the roofs red.

10. Color $1/12$ of the bottom part of the houses red.

11. Color $3/12$ ($1/4$) of the bottom part of the houses green.

12. Draw a sidewalk in front of $2/12$ ($1/6$) of the houses.

13. Write your name above $1/12$ of the houses.

14. Write today's date below $1/12$ of the houses.

Houses

Reproducible for use with page 73.

Answer Key

Ladybugs, title page

Pre/Posttest, Part 1, page 2

(Name in top right corner.)

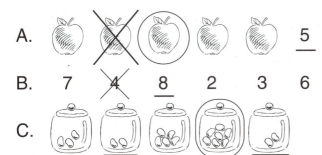

A. $\underline{5}$

B.   7   ✗4 $\underline{8}$ 2   3   6

C.

D.   9, 12, 3, 25, 36, 17, 48

E.   2, 6, 9, 12, 15, 18

F. $\underline{36}$ (129)   71   4   265

G.   66

One to Ten, page 3

Front

Back

Find the Number, page 3

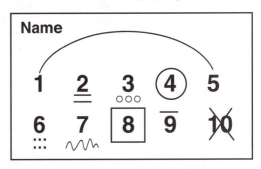

Window Shopping, page 4

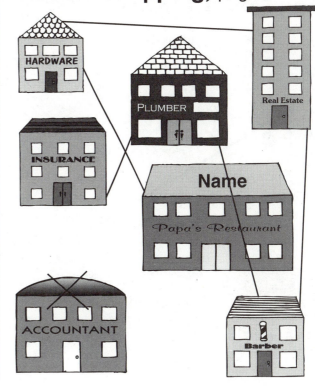

Colored Windows, page 4

(Outcomes may vary slightly.)
R = red   B = blue
G = green   Y = yellow

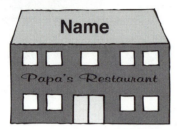

HARDWARE (Y)

PLUMBER (G)

Real Estate

B	Y
B	Y
B	Y
B	Y
B	Y

INSURANCE (R R R / R R R / R R)

Name — Papa's Restaurant

ACCOUNTANT (R)

Barber (B)

Egg Count 1, page 6

Name

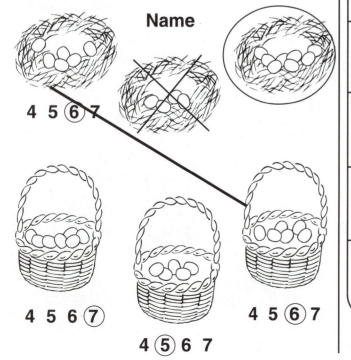

4 5 ⑥ 7

4 5 6 ⑦   4 ⑤ 6 7   4 5 ⑥ 7

Egg Count 2, page 7

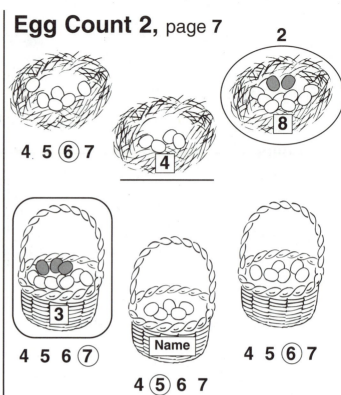

2

8

4 5 ⑥ 7   4

4 5 6 ⑦   4 ⑤ 6 7   4 5 ⑥ 7

3

Name

Colored Clues, page 9

O = orange   B = brown
G = green   R = red
Y = yellow

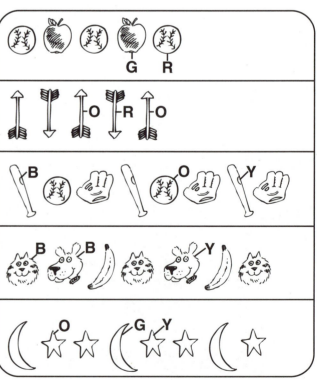

G   R

↑O   ↑R   ↑O

B   O   Y

B   B   Y

O   G Y

Ⓝame

TLC10005 Copyright © Teaching & Learning Company, Carthage, IL 62321

Numbered Boxes, page 11

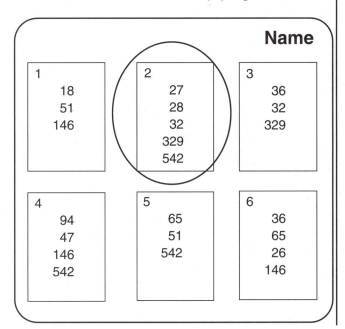

Name

1	2	3
18 51 146	27 28 32 329 542	36 32 329

4	5	6
94 47 146 542	65 51 542	36 65 26 146

Count Up, Count Down, page 12

(Name in top left corner.)

2. 6, 13, 15, 18
3. 4, 8, 13, 17, 21, 25, 32, 36, 40, 44, 47
4. 56, 62, 70, 78, 84, 90, 96
5. 25, 50, 65, 90
6. 18, 15, 11, 8, 4
7. 95, 75, 50, 20
8. 46, 40, 32, 26, 18, 12, 6

Number Hunt 1, page 13

(Name in top right corner.)

1	2	3	4	5	6	7	8	9	10
11	12	13	14	15	16	17	18	19	20
21	22	23	24	25	26	27	28	29	30
31	32	33	34	35	36	37	38	39	40
41	42	43	44	45	46	47	48	49	50

Number Hunt 2, page 14

(Name below chart.)

1	2	3	4	5	6	7	8	9	10
11	12̄	13	14	15	16	17	18	19	20
21	22	23	24	25	26	27	28	29	30
31	32	33	34	35	36	37	38	39	�40
㊶	㊷	㊸	㊹	㊺	㊻	㊼	㊽	㊾	50
51	52	53	54	55	56	57	58	59	60
61	62	63	64	65	66	67	68	69	70
71	72	73	74	75̲	76	77	78	79	80
81	82	83̲	84	85	86	87	88	89	90
91	92	93	94	95	96	97̄	98	99	100

Columns, page 16

(Name at top of page.)

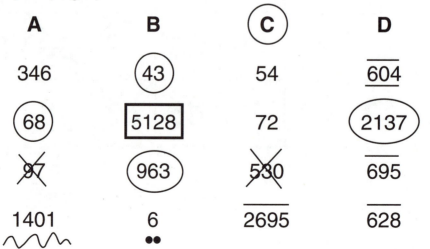

A	B	©	D
346	㊸43	54	6̄04
⓺8	⊡5128	72	⬭2137
9̶7̶	⬭963	5̶3̶0̶	6̄95
1401	6	2̄695	6̄28

78

TLC10005 Copyright © Teaching & Learning Company, Carthage, IL 62321

Even–Odd, page 18

1. 1, 3, 5
2. 12, 14, 16, 18
3. 22, 24, 26
4. 41, 43, 45, 47, 49
5. 97, 99
6. Any 4 of these: 2, 4, 6, 8, 10, 12, 14, 16, 18
7. Any 3 of these: 81, 83, 85, 87, 89
8. 26
9. 72
10. 7
11. 91
12. Answers will vary.

Pre/Posttest, Part 2, page 20

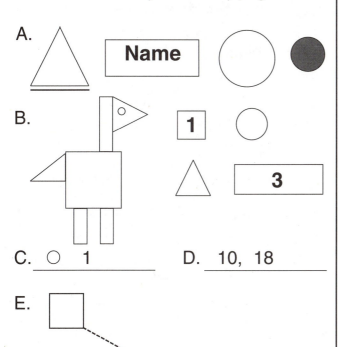

A.

B.

C. ○ 1   D. 10, 18

E.

Clown Face, page 21

Folded Shapes, page 22

(One other edge will also be folded.)

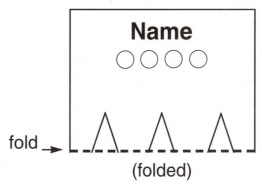

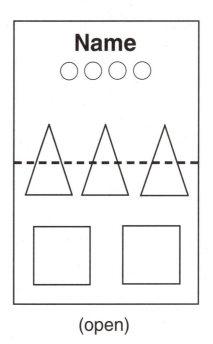

Shape Caper, page 22

R = red   B = blue

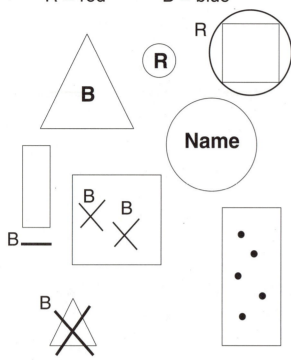

Shape Search, page 24

R = red   B = blue   G = green

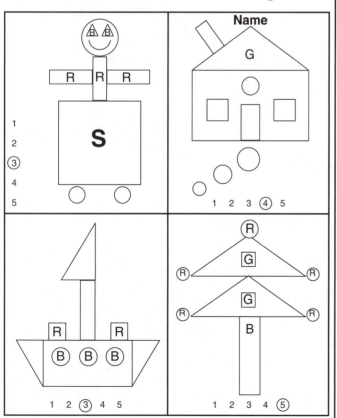

Shapely Details, page 26

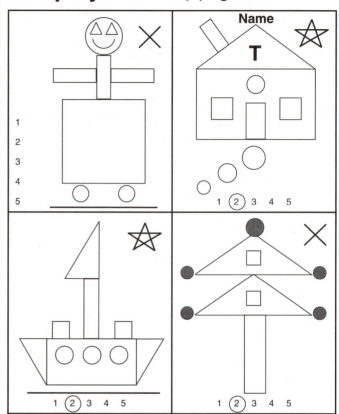

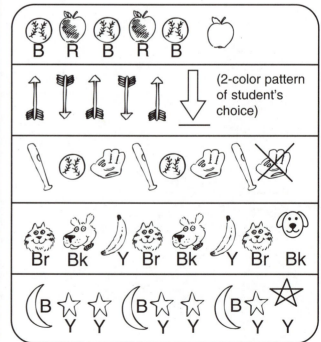

Colored Patterns, page 27

R = red   B = blue   Y = yellow
Bk = black   Br = brown

Name

B	R	B	R	B	

(2-color pattern of student's choice)

Br	Bk	Y	Br	Bk	Y	Br	Bk

B	Y	Y	B	Y	Y	B	Y	Y

What's Next?, page 28

1. square
2. tree
3. sun
4. 2
5. ball
6. 2
7. cat
8. L
9. hat
10. Pattern of student's choice using own name.

Baseball, page 30

(Slight variations are possible.)

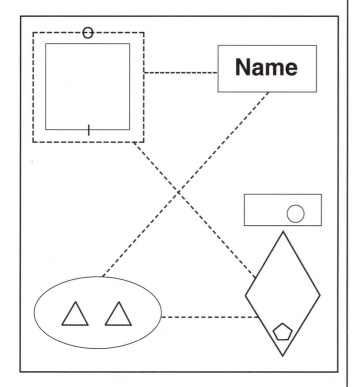

What's Missing?, page 31

(Name in top right corner.)

1. 12
2. 25, 40
3. April, October
4. 11, 17
5. Thursday
6. hundreds
7. sixth
8. 17, 13
9. dimes
10. 80, 65

Pre/Posttest, Part 3, page 32

(Name in top right corner.)

1. 2, 1, 5
2. 4
3. (6 4)   5 4   3 8
4. 14
5. 8, 8, 9
6. down, 4
7. 7, S
8.
$$\begin{array}{r} 96 \\ -\ 34 \\ \hline \cancel{52} \end{array}$$
9. 529   241   706
$$\begin{array}{r} 706 \\ +\ 241 \\ \hline 947 \end{array}$$
10.
$$\begin{array}{r} 863 \\ -\ 529 \\ \hline 334 \end{array} \qquad \begin{array}{r} 617 \\ -\ 132 \\ \hline 485 \end{array}$$

(One problem should have an X next to it.)

Adam's Apples, page 34

Ten Sums, page 35

(Name at bottom of page.)

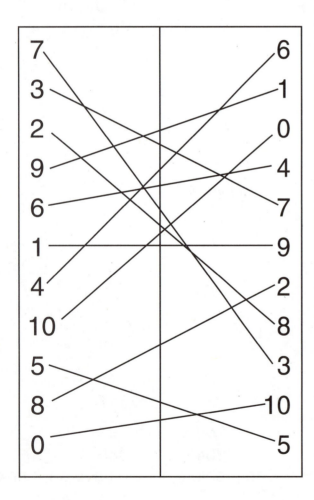

Score More, page 35

(Name in top left corner.)

1. 16	6. 12
2. 14	7. 14
3. 16	8. 13
4. 13	9. 18
5. 14	10. 13

Add the Signs, page 36

(Name in top right corner.)

A.
$$\begin{array}{cccccc} 3 & 4 & 5 & 3 & 4 & 4 \\ +1 & +3 & +1 & +0 & +4 & +2 \\ \hline 4 & 7 & 6 & 3 & 8 & 6 \end{array}$$

B.
$$\begin{array}{cccccc} 5 & 3 & 5 & 4 & 5 & 2 \\ -0 & -2 & -4 & -1 & -3 & -1 \\ \hline 5 & 1 & 1 & 3 & 2 & 1 \end{array}$$
(3, 5, and 2 columns circled)

C.
$$\begin{array}{cccccc} 1 & 3 & 5 & 4 & 2 & 0 \\ +1 & -3 & +5 & -4 & +2 & -0 \\ \hline 2 & 0 & 10 & 0 & 4 & 0 \end{array}$$

Speedy Subtraction, page 38

(Name in top left corner.)

1. 9	13. 4
2. 9	14. 9
3. 3	15. 6
4. 8	16. 9
5. 5	17. 8
6. 6	18. 3
7. 4	19. 8
8. 6	20. 9
9. 8	21. 8
10. 7	22. 9
11. 7	23. 7
12. 7	24. 8

Ups and Downs, page 39

1. down, 7°, name
2. up, $2
3. up, $10
4. down, 7 students
5. up, 5 newspapers
6. down, 4 marbles
7. up, 4 people
8. down, 10 birds
9. down, 9 stories
10. up, 3 squares

Scoreboard, page 40

Hawks

Inning	1	2	3	4	5	6	7	Total
Hits	0	2	7	0	4	4	1	18
Runs	0	0	3	0	2	2	0	7

Caps

Inning	1	2	3	4	5	6	7	Total
Hits	3	2	2	0	2	2	6	17
Runs	1	0	1	0	1	1	4	8

(Caps) 8

Hawks 18

Name

Oops!, page 41

(Name in top left corner.)

First row:
$$24 + 42 = 66$$
$$(15 + 83 = 97)$$
$$(21 + 34 = 45)$$
$$84 + 14 = 98$$
98   55

Second row:
$$78 - 20 = 48$$
$$(37 + 42 = 49)$$
$$96 - 34 = 51$$
$$(16 + 63 = 78)$$
58   79   62   79

Third row:
$$89 - 54 = 45$$
$$76 - 31 = 44$$
$$50 - 20 = 30$$
$$64 - 31 = 33$$
35   45

Chalkboard Challenge, page 42

(Name in top right corner.)

1. 614
2. 897
3. 864
4. 121
5. 909
6. 826
7. 296
8. 767
9. 966
10. 659

Three-Digit Doodles, page 43

Shown are answers to problems. Circled problems will vary from student to student.
(Name in top right corner.)

A.
$$396 + 412 = 808$$
$$708 + 133 = 841$$
$$614 + 416 = 1{,}030$$
$$324 + 140 = 464$$

B.
$$168 + 591 = 759$$
$$890 + 346 = 1{,}236$$
$$705 + 434 = 1{,}139$$
$$281 + 243 = 524$$

C.
$$429 - 36 = 393$$
$$652 - 507 = 145$$
$$735 - 180 = 555$$
$$267 - 35 = 232$$

D. Answers for the two problems in this row will vary.

Pre/Posttest, Part 4, page 45

Name

A.

B. __6__

C. 4 x __3__ = 12

5 x __3__ = 15

7 x __2__ = 14

D. Sue __13¢__   Tom __20¢__

E.

16	17	~~18~~	19	20
26	27	(28)	29	30

Pet Pals, page 47

Each dog should have 3 bones.
Each mouse should have 3 pieces
of cheese. Each kitten should have
2 balls. Two birds should be at
each feeder. Student's name
should be at bottom of page.

Multiple Stories, page 49

(Name in top left corner.)

1. 4   6. 10
2. 6   7. $3
3. 16   8. 6
4. 8   9. 12
5. 9

Line Up, page 50

(Name in top right corner.)

4 x 2 =   8

1 x 5 =   5

5 x 3 = 15

2 x 3 =   6

3 x 4 = 12

(4 x 4 = 16)

5 x 2 = 10

(3 x 3 =   9)

(2 x 2 =   4)

1 x 0 =   0

4 x 5 = 20

(5 x 5 = 25)

Candy Shop, page 51

(Name at top of page.)

1. Tasha, 9¢
2. Gary, 11¢
3. Ann, 10¢
4. (Lee,) 25¢
5. Amy, 13¢
6. Omar, 11¢
7. Ed, 20¢
8. Jill, 17¢
9. Rob, 17¢

Colored Products, page 52

R = red   B = blue   G = green   Y = yellow   Bk = black   Br = brown

(Name in top right corner.)

1	2	3	4	5	6	7	8	9	10
11	~~12~~ (G/Br)	13	**14** (Bk)	15	~~16~~ (R)	17	<u>18</u> (G)	19	<u>20</u> (R)
(21) (Bk)	22	23	**24** (R)	25	26	27	~~28~~ (Br)	29	(30) (Y)
31	32	33	34	(35) (G)	<u>36</u> (B)	37	38	39	40
41	(42) (B)	43	44	45	46	47	48	**49** (Y)	50

Pre/Posttest, Part 5, page 53

(Answers may vary slightly on A.)

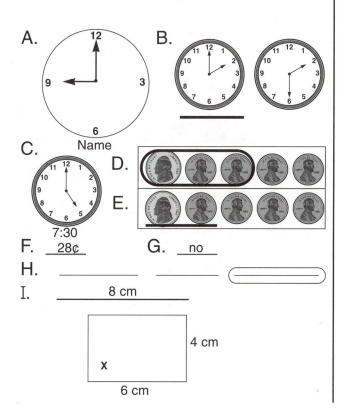

A.

B.

C.

D.

E.

F.   28¢   G.   no

H. _____   (   )

I. _____ 8 cm

4 cm
x
6 cm

Time to Draw, page 56

Name

Hour Time, page 57

R = red   B = blue
G = green   Y = yellow

Name

A.
B.
C.

D.
E.
F.

G.
H.
I.

J.
K.
L.

Time to Add, page 59

A.
B. **Name**
C.

D.  7:30
E. 6:30
F. 9:30

G. 5:30
H. 8:00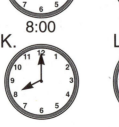
I. 2:00 ... 3:00

J.
K.
L.

Coin Count, page 60

(Name at top of paper.)

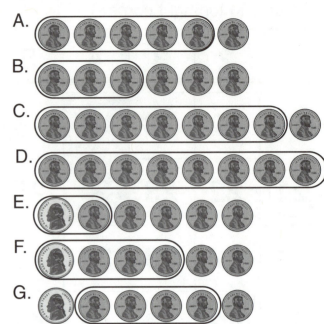

Coin Math, page 61   **Name**

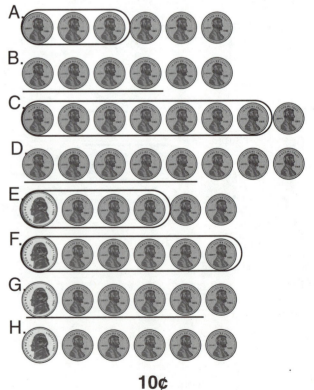

10¢

TLC10005 Copyright © Teaching & Learning Company, Carthage, IL 62321

Betsy's Birthday, page 63

37¢

Name

Bonus: 1. under a coaster
2. under the doormat

Coin Comparison, page 64

(Name at top left of page.)

1. yes
2. yes
3. no
4. yes
5. 40¢
6. 49¢
7. C
8. B
9. J
10. B

Inchworms, page 65

Br = brown   Y = yellow   B = blue

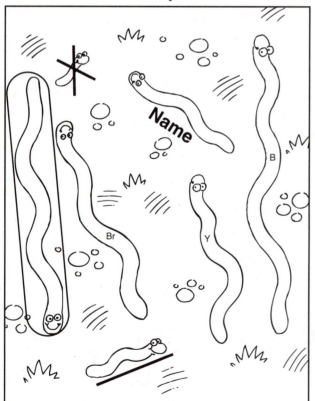

Centimeter Draw, page 65

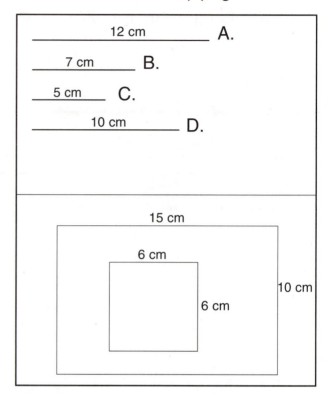

X Marks the Spot, page 67

This page should look approximately like this:

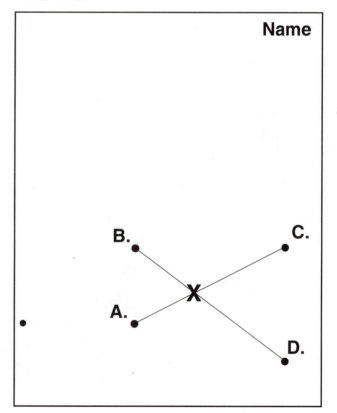

Pre/Posttest, Part 6, page 68

(Answers may vary slightly.)

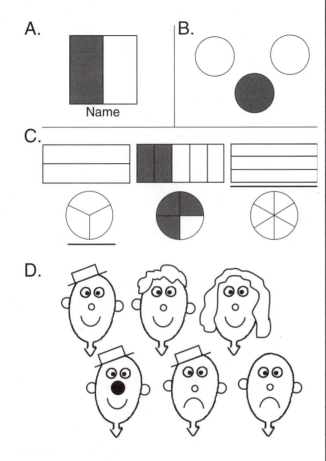

A.

B.

Name

C.

D.

Fraction Draw, page 71

(Variations are possible.)

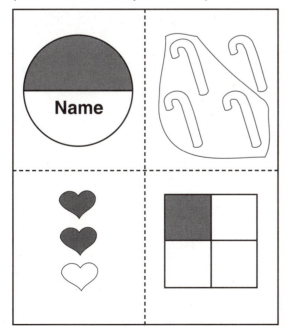

Name

Fractured Shapes, page 71

(Variations are possible.)

X

Name

X

X

X

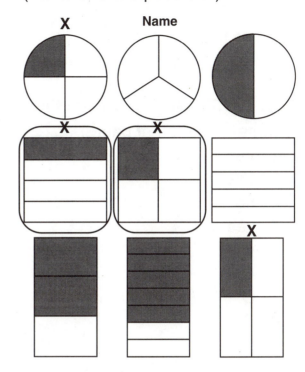

Home Improvements, page 73

(Outcomes may vary greatly.)

Here is one correct solution.

R = red   G = green

Name

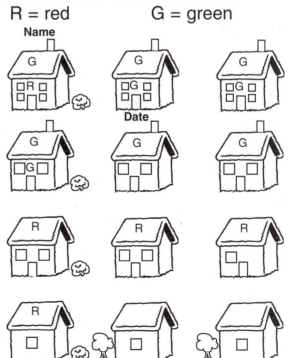

Date